SINGLED IN

2nd Edition

Your Mate Awaits

Jeffrey Lee Brothers

Chocolate Donut Publishing
Nashville, TN

First edition © 2014 Jeffrey Lee Brothers
Second edition © 2016 Jeffrey Lee Brothers

Published by Chocolate Donut Publishing
135 Hermitage Woods Drive
Hermitage, TN 37076

Printed in the United States of America

All rights reserved. No part of this publication may be reproduced, stored in a retrieval system, or transmitted in any form or by any means – for example, electronic, photocopy, and recording – without the prior written permission of the publisher. The only exception is brief quotations in written reviews.

ISBN-13: 978-1500886981

ISBN-10: 150088698x

Scripture quotations identified as ASV are from the American Standard Version of the Bible.

Scripture quotations identified as KJV are from the King James Version of the Bible.

Cover design:
Terri Morris @ Mollie B. Art
Nashville, TN
http://molliebcreative.blogspot.com

Endorsements

"I've had the privilege of knowing Jeff Brothers for almost 20 years, during which his singleness has both perplexed and challenged me. I've seen him balance ardent anticipation for marriage with total contentment with singleness in a way like none other, and I am overjoyed that he is finally sharing his trade secrets of successful singleness with others. "Singled In" is pure genius. It is the cure for lonely singleness, and sets a new standard for the proper pursuit of marriage and most importantly, for right relationship with God." - **Laura Harris Smith, #1 Best-selling author of *Seeing the Voice of God: What God is Telling You Through Dreams and Visions*** (Chosen Books, 2014)

"First, Jeff Brothers has written an important book for the Body of Christ. Second, it is a lot of fun to read. Great personal stories and humor make "Singled In" one of those books you want to read straight through. Along the way, Jeff provides a fresh and original approach for ministering to the singles in our congregations. Great read for small group leaders in particular." - **J. Benz, Worship Pastor New Life Community Church, Louisa VA**

"As a participant in the single journey, I cannot agree more with the "Singled In" approach. Your relationship with the One who puts the breath in your lungs is the greatest and most important relationship in your life-married or unmarried. "Singled In" beautifully paints the picture for singles to live an active and purposeful life because we, too, have been called by God to live a life that is pleasing to Him. I highly recommend this book to you-no matter what your relationship status is." – **Jeorgi Smith, Executive Director (her•story) Women's Ministries, Nashville TN**

See more glowing endorsements at Singled-in.net

Dedication & Acknowledgements

- Pastors Chris and Laura Smith; and my church body Eastgate Creative Christian Fellowship; for encouraging me to stand up in public and preach this message.

  http://www.eastgateccf.com/#/im-new/watch
  episode 6

- Rick Meyer for developing e-Sword. Your incredible application made researching the Bible efficient and effective.

  www.e-sword.com

- David Sluka and Hit the Mark School of Publishing, whose Nashville seminar inspired me to finish this work and take it to the next level.

  http://david-sluka.com

Why a 2nd Edition?

The idea that gave birth to the first *Singled In* book has not changed. In fact, not much inside the covers has changed at all in this new edition - a few menial structure issues. But, as *Singled In* enthusiasts will no doubt notice, the cover and sub-title are totally different.

As readers and prospective readers responded to *Singled In* back in 2014, I began noticing a recurring sentiment. It revolved around the sub-title, *Finding Fulfillment in the Unmarried Life*.

I'll codify; "Your book would be great if I didn't mind being single for the rest of my life. But, I want to get married some day."

Ugh, the mark had been missed. This "wanna get married" mindset was one of several the author attempted to draw to his pages to minister the soothing and enlightening words of his fantastic book. However, to do that, one must make the leap past the cover (and the sub-title).

Unfortunately for publishers in today's market, it is nearly impossible not to judge the book by the cover. So, we re-thought, re-grouped, re-doubled and, in the spirit of drawing more bees with honey, put a pretty girl and a catchy phrase as our new sub-title! And, here you are reading the creamy nougat filling on the inside of the crunchy eye-candy coating. The great thing is, there are no calories, it tastes great and it will change your life for the better!

The *Singled In* message: Life in God and His Kingdom is the way to find what you are looking for. With that in mind, prior to each of the four section headings, you will notice various uses of the word "mate."

Your Mate Awaits is more than just a catchy phrase. Studying some of the different uses of the word "mate" helps illustrate the *Singled In* message.

Wherever you are along God's timeline for your life, there is always a mate awaiting to help you with your heart's desire. It's also good to remember that spending time with your first mate, [your first love (1 John 4:19)], will make the relationships with all your other mates better. - Jeffrey

SINGLED IN

2nd *Edition*

Your Mate Awaits

Contents

Introduction   **16**

PART ONE – What Am I Doing Here?

**Chapter 1: The Definition:
Singled In**   **21**

Being *Singled In* is more about living and less about dating.

1. Brother Bill's Bungle
2. Tradition is straining

**Chapter 2: The Contrast:
Singled Out vs. Singled In**   **28**

Today's non-nuclear families are crying for more

a. Dating
b. New wineskin

Chapter 3: The Need   **36**

Be a participator, not a spectator

1. I Need You
2. Participation, Not "Spectation"

Chapter 4: The Goal   **40**

Don't settle for "good enough." Go for "awesome!"

1. Alpha-I-Omega Fraternity
2. God's Will
3. Mama's Christmas tree
4. God's "good" will
5. God's "acceptable" will
6. God's "perfect" will

<u>PART TWO</u>: Focus on the person, not the need

Chapter 5: The Identity   **51**

Break the smoky mirror

    a. Personal testimony
    b. Justification-ism

Chapter 6: The Numbers   **57**

100 million Elvis fans can't be wrong

    a. Terminology needs updating
    b. US census numbers
    c. Dating services

Chapter 7: The New Identity   **61**

Wait...what?!

    a. The Balcony Story

b. More Lord
   c. Ch-ch-ch-changes
   d. On a mission
   e. A new beginning

Chapter 8: The Longing   76

Loneliness is a call to action

   a. Prayer
   b. God Uses Loneliness
   c. The First Family
   d. The First Church
   e. Bachelor Auction Story

PART THREE: Discovering self by helping others

Chapter 9: The Fulfillment   96

Everyone is created with a desire for something more

   a. Fulfillment vs. Feeling
   b. Plateaus

Chapter 10: The Purpose   104

No fulfillment without purpose

   a. MORE is better
   b. True Life is Science Fiction
   c. Feed My Sheep

Chapter 11: The Challenge   109

Life is hard

    a. Judas Is Scary, Yes?
    b. Jesus Applied
    c. Glorified

PART FOUR: "Singleness" is an opportunity

Chapter 12: The Implementation   118

Positively influence your community

    a. Simple act of service
    b. Point Person
    c. Idea 0
    d. Idea 1
    e. Idea 2
    f. Idea 3

Chapter 13: The Illusion   128

Is marriage an illusion?

    a. Godly Disillusionment
    b. Synergy
    c. Fear and Discouragement
    d. A Good Thing
    e. The One

Chapter 14: The Advantages   **141**

Paul calls it "a gift"

> a. Accentuate the Positive
> b. Unmarried Bible Characters
> c. Better Than Marriage

Chapter 15: The Sex and the Sin   **149**

Premarital sex is fun

> a. But, if we love each other...
> b. Cause to Celebrate
> c. Purity
> d. Purpose of Sex
> e. I Can't Wait
> f. Adultery – Plain and Simple
> g. Sin Misses the Mark

Chapter 16: The Conclusion   **170**

Being single is a gift – not a curse

> a. *Singled In* is a mindset
> b. Our Lady of the Hard Head

INTRODUCTION

You picked up this book while searching for something else, didn't you? You didn't really want to spend the money on another "thing." You would much rather just obtain that hard-to-describe something that is missing in your life. Me too. I would much rather just magically dwell within the confines of this nearly tangible something than to write this book, too. But as we're told, "it's the journey, not the destination."

I must admit, as hard as it is to do so, I don't know everything. Before writing this book I did. But now, I'm happy to tell you that I don't. It's a freeing experience to allow your ego to take a vacation...and then another...and another, until the fool thing has moved away entirely. It still likes to visit, but I don't put out the good china any longer.

This journey that you and I are on to fill our empty places is very common. So common, in fact, that all of us are currently on at least one. Many of us are on several journeys simultaneously trying to keep all our junk from falling out of the overstuffed station wagon. (Note to self: Next book should be about simplifying one's journey. Got it.)

Before my ego took it's first extended vacation, I ignored my journey and kept looking toward my destination. I wanted to arrive at a place of fulfillment. I had packed the vision, the means and the medium. All I thought I needed was to find my mode.

You may not be as stubborn as I. It took many, many years to get the blinders off my goal-oriented eyes. Perhaps you just have an empty-ish feeling and you're not quite sure what it is or what to do about it. It's my hope that my many exploits and mistakes used to extol the virtues of being *Singled In* will, at least, show you what <u>not</u> to do and make your search more rewarding much more quickly than mine.

As you will see, my vision of what would fill my heart with happiness and purpose led me down some strange and sometimes amusing paths. I was determined that the right girl, the right job and a family would soothe my soul. I would plant my flag, build my life and enjoy the fire out of it, so get out of my way or get run over!

Life kept rearranging my plans, however. Does that happen to you? What I continue to realize is that life is much larger in scope than my myopia will allow me to see. There is a bigger plan. Yes, it includes me. Guess what? It includes you, too. Yep, the big plan I am in has you in it, too! Let's jump in and get *Singled In* together!

"I will make him an help meet* for him."

Genesis 2:18b KJV

*meet – Hebrew 5828, **'êzer***, ay'zer; aid - help*

**PART ONE
WHAT AM I DOING HERE?**

1

The Definition *Singled In*

More about living and less about dating

Each unmarried person has a purpose and a destiny. *Singled In* weaves unmarried people into the fabric of their community to serve and be served. That's really all there is to it.

All along the *Singled In* highway, many destination on-ramps will be revealed. But, some of those on-ramps need repair. There are also some construction zones that should be avoided entirely.

Let's listen in to a Valentine's Day church service that should open your eyes to a few potholes along our freeway.

<u>Brother Bill's Bungle</u>
"Good morning brothers and sisters, neighbors, friends and visitors. I am Brother Bill Williamson and I'd like to

welcome you to the First Bapticostal Presby-Luthern Church of the Holy Sepulcher of Jesus Christ and All His Saints in Glory – with and without snakes. Whew! It's a glorious Valentine's Day morning here in God's country. I'm sure you married folk have blessed each other with a holy kiss in remembrance of St. Valentine. Brother Ron…that means <u>your</u> wife. Ha ha…yes. Well now, I'd like to recognize all of you single people out there…would you please stand and let us have a good look at you? I wanna point y'all out so we can pray for you."

The unmarried people in the congregation stand.

"Whoa! There's more of y'all than I thought. I'd better pray big."

(A whispered voice over cuts in, not unlike a play-by-play sportscaster in golf.)

In the midst of the congregation during Brother Bill's prayer, a murmur swells as ears are bent to the whispers of duly self-appointed matchmakers. A softly spoken name is barely audible.

"Joan"

No answer

A little louder this time, "Joan"

"What, Nadine!?"

"Do you see who's a-standin' up?"

"Who?" Nadine turns to take a cursory look around.

"Don't look!"

Nadine snaps back to attention with eyes darting side-to-side.

"It's Jeffrey. I didn't know he was still single. How do you expect that happened?"

"Shameful"

"You see who else is standin' in the back?"

"No, I..." Out of habit, Nadine again starts the turn.

"Don't look!"

"It's Darlene."

"Oh, Joanie, we need to set up a little dinner party."

"Nadine, now you know that'll go over like a pregnant pole-vaulter. Just leave well enough alone."

"Oh, ye of little faith. Keep next Saturday night open and let me work my magic."

Standing at the 9th pew on the right hand side of the pulpit, Jeffrey thinks to himself, "Dang! This is embarrassing, but it <u>is</u> great advertising. I wonder if it would be too obvious if I just slowly turned around and took a peak at the dating pool."

Remember, this is a totally fictional account and it is sheer coincidence that the embarrassed guy standing at the 9th pew has the same name as the author of this book.

Illustration by: Brian Frost

Tradition is Straining

Poor Brother Bill means well. He is trying to meet the needs of this group in his congregation and is using time-tested means to do so. He "singled out" certain churchgoers and shined the spotlight brightly upon each when he asked them to stand. Those standing can't help but feel scrutinized, pitied or, at worst, denigrated for their perceived plight. Brother Bill had the best of intentions as he wished to acknowledge those singles in his body and encourage them in their walk with the Lord. But, what he meant for good actually opened wide a door for others in his flock to attempt to do God's work for Him.

Of course, this fictional church body is not representative of your church body, right? I'm sure, under the same circumstances; your folk would see all of those standing singles for who they are in Christ Jesus, right? Your folk would encourage them, pray for them, walk with them and let the Lord do His work in them in His timing, right? Your church doesn't have God-helpers like Brother Bill, Nadine or Joan. Good. I thought so.

Due to the sheer increase in numbers of unmarried people in the past few years, the traditional "Singled Out" approach is straining its reach and, therefore, losing its effectiveness. That's where *Singled In* can make a difference. It can augment and help any existing structure or even stand-alone as a ministry model.

2

The Contrast:
Singled Out
Vs.
Singled In

Today's non-nuclear families are crying for more

The common method used by churches and civic groups to serve their unmarried members is one illustrated by Brother Bill in Chapter 1. We've deemed it the "Singled Out" approach. It serves singles by separating them from the rest of the general population. (Wow, did I really just use a prison term there? Gen-pop?) Let's press on.

Having never married, I have been involved with several church singles ministries, some civic groups and even a few private groups. Some, I would say, successfully met the common needs of the participants. A few...eh...well...let's be nice and say they fell a little short in some areas and leave it at that. Each had its own flavor, but all shared a similar approach. That approach was to treat a group of unmarried folks as a distinct population segment and to serve it as a whole. By doing so, the participants were usually separated from the rest of the church or community.

Dating

This "singled out" approach uses a Sunday school or day care template, where kids of certain age groups gather for learning and fellowship. On the surface, doing a singles group this way seems perfectly natural. There are probably many participants who have grown up in Sunday school or day care together. So far, so good.

But, gathering co-ed singles together after puberty kicks in and hormones start flowing can become a challenge to squeeze any learning past the fellowship. The dating dynamic forces its way into the equation. In fact, in the common "singled out" approach, where participants are grouped together by age and do singles-only events, a single person is almost always interacting with other single people. The dating dynamic is nearly always in play.

Let me clarify something. The term "dating" as we use in contemporary society is not productive in the kingdom of God. "Dating" puts each person in the center of his/her own self-gratification universe. The result is each potential "date" becomes a test of how one can use the other to best please oneself. Or, at least it is a test of will power – neither is a strong Christian principle.

This is not to say that good Christian people should not date. But contemporary dating introduces many, many temptations that challenge purity and can wilt even the strongest of wills. For this reason, there is a growing interest in Victorian-era courting again.

Josh Harris lays out a best-case scenario in his pro-courting book, *I Kissed Dating Goodbye*. His mantra is to "Walk shoulder-to-shoulder with one another, doing good, until, naturally, you begin to turn to each other face-to-face."[1] This mindset honors each person as "betrothed to God alone" until there is a marriage to an earthly spouse. In this way the couple is both protected and respected by each other and their community.

No matter how you plan to pursue a co-ed relationship, it's always good to have defined parameters and discuss those with your date and the parents before toddling off into a relationship.

Any good singles group leader can tell you that the biggest challenge is to remove or drastically minimize the dating dynamic from the group. From experience, I can say that no matter what the median age or maturity level of the group of single people, the dating dynamic is always present. Singles leaders: Teach respect. Teach modesty. Teach kingdom-focus. "For with God nothing shall be impossible."[2]

<u>New wineskin</u>
The twentieth century saw modern society begin an upswing in its assault upon the traditional family unit. The barrage

has only increased with time. The result is more and more unmarried people in all demographic segments. Many, over one third of U.S. adults (that's over 100 million!), find themselves to be single or single again. Some singles don't even identify themselves with that word, "single," because they have children living at home. They are more inclined to consider themselves unmarried or divorced. So, singles are searching for their identities, fulfillment and purpose in just about every nook and cranny the world has to offer. There is a better way.

I already mentioned that being *Singled In* is more about living and less about dating. Let's also add that being *Singled In* <u>IN</u>-cludes unmarrieds inside and outside the walls of buildings. What does that mean, exactly?

God designed life on earth to be lived interactively with many different types of people.

Singled In is simply the involvement of the unmarried population into non-segregated community life. As these single folks interact with others - married or not, the feelings of self esteem and self worth grow, while the needs of all participants are served. This method can be used by anyone in any social setting, especially church, regardless of group size or location.

Singled In is not a program, although it can be implemented as one. It is, however, a mindset – one, which can use some cheer leading in this day and time. Brother Bill would certainly benefit from a little sit-down chat on the subject.

Of the 100 million single people in the US, if we were to take an arbitrary cross section, you would see a long range of ages and needs. Even as the groups are brought down to the local level for personalized service, it is nearly impossible to serve all those needs without forsaking some.

Larger communities and churches can combat this challenge by breaking its large singles population into age-defined sub-groups of 20's, 30's, 40's, etc. I have seen this approach work to great affect. Woo Hoo! Way to go!

I hear you thinking, "But, my assembly is small and we don't have the luxury of workers or resources to lead multiple groups." Or, "what about my group whose charismatic leader moved away and the remaining workers are looking for a way to keep the fire burning?"

Whether you are an unmarried person looking for fulfillment; love such a person; or are looking to energize your church or civic group's service to singles, *Singled In* is for you.

3

The Need

Be a participator, not a spectator

I Need You

So, who needs to be *Singled In*? Why <u>you</u>, of course – if you are an unmarried person, who finds himself or herself living life with little help, you need me. I need you. We need each other. God built families, clans, nations and His church to meet the needs of the members. There are many flavors to these institutions out there. And, the fact that you are reading this book suggests that you have tried a few of these flavors to satisfy your hunger for fulfillment – physical, emotional or spiritual.

Participation, not "Spectation"

Church can be a great place to find the fulfillment you are looking for. But, to find that fulfillment, interaction is required. There are just as many married folks feeling the same things you are. You can single yourself into their situations. Ask if you can tag along with the family for lunch. Boom! You're *singled in*. That suggestion is free of charge. There are more in Chapter 12, but they cost extra.

Church, Biblically defined, is not a religion or a building - admittedly, the definitional lines can get grayed if you're not careful. Church is actually defined as a "body of Christian believers." So, the <u>church is the people</u> who show up in the building (and other functions) and hang out together.

Another thing church isn't, it is <u>not</u> a spectator sport. You cannot find fulfillment by just occupying a seat in a sanctuary on Sunday morning. While Jesus gave gifts of salvation, grace, love, mercy, joy, peace, etc. unconditionally free of charge to you and I, Jesus wants all to receive these gifts. He wants you and I to show others these gifts, so they will want them, too. "But we have this treasure in earthen vessels, that the exceeding greatness of the power may be of God, and not from ourselves."[3]

What I'm getting at is that, it is up to you, dear reader, to take some initiative in your quest for fulfillment. Reading this book is a good move in the right direction.

You may show up week after week amongst the same people and sit in the same seat, but unless you open yourself up to share a little of your life with someone else, the fulfillment you seek will evade you. Being vulnerable with trusted others challenges and grows all involved.

Photo credit: Jeffrey Lee Brothers

4

The Goal

Don't settle for "good enough." Go for "awesome!"

"And be not fashioned according to this world: but be ye transformed by the renewing of your mind, and ye may prove what is the good and acceptable and perfect will of God."[4]

<u>Alpha-I-Omega Fraternity</u>

So, what is our goal with a *Singled In* mindset? Is it to stave off loneliness or fix a broken heart? How 'bout to meet physical needs? Or, is it to foster spiritual growth?

The *Singled In* mindset shines the light of God upon the truth of Jesus, so that everyone involved will experience the person of Jesus. Since being a "Christian" means "belonging to a brotherhood of Christ followers," interaction is not only key, it is assumed.   Being *Singled In* means that, as an unmarried person, you will be interacting with, sharing with, being helped by and helping other unmarried and married people.

In a ministry to single persons, Jesus mends many broken hearts. But, should this be His main function? As amazing as this function of His/our ministry to each other is, I believe it is a foundation upon which larger things can be built. Jesus can bind up broken hearts until the cows come home, but life is more than triage. He came "...that they might have life, and that they might have *it* more abundantly."[5] Abundant life...yep, that sounds like what I'm looking for.

Every person, single or not, is "...to be conformed (formed, shaped) into the image of His Son..."[6] Any singles ministry should hold this banner high with every event, sermon, teaching and communication falling under it.

There are some who would believe that the goal of a singles ministry is to get its members wed. Sure, marriage is an admirable goal. I'm not belittling it at all. However, it should not be venerated at the expense of singleness. The Apostle Paul suggests that being single is a blessing unto itself. We'll talk more about that a little later.

<u>Any</u> service to <u>any</u> person should focus on the relationship between that person and Jesus. As that relationship blossoms, so too will many other relationships. Jesus sacrificed so we would have a relationship with His father. As an unmarried person then, we should "seek [sic] first the Kingdom of God and His righteousness" and watch while "all these (other) things (like marriage, kids, family) shall be added unto (us)."[7]

<u>God's Will</u>

Before we move any further along in the process of integrating singles into the community at large, let's take a look at the verse quoted at the beginning of this chapter - Romans 12:2. This verse spells out the goal of any ministry, including *Singled In*. "And be not conformed to this world: but be ye transformed by the renewing of your mind, that ye may prove what *is* that good, and acceptable, and perfect, will of God."[8]

In his letter to the Christians in first century Rome, Paul seems to be making a distinction here. For years, I read through Romans 12:2 with an emphasis on the transformation of one's mind - that by spending time with God, I would be able to discern His will.

This is a workable interpretation of the verse, but, upon closer examination, there is more depth. Look again and see that there are actually three levels to God's will – good, acceptable and perfect. By looking at the Greek definitions of these words, we can see a clear delineation. God's "good" will is defined as that, which is beneficial. His "acceptable" will is one, which is well pleasing to Him. God's "perfect" will is that, which completes the work – completeness.

Mama's Christmas Tree

To illustrate the 3-fold will of God in Romans 12, let's look at a Christmas tree.

Mama has invited the entire family over for Christmas dinner. All of the kids, grandkids and extended family have confirmed their attendance. So, Mama wants everything to be like a postcard. She gives Daddy the task of procuring the centerpiece of this once-in-a-lifetime family holiday.

God's "Good" Will

The tasking of the tree to Daddy occurred week one of December. Increasingly un-subtle reminders continued as days passed with no tree in the foyer.

Christmas eve arrives and the foyer still has no tree. Daddy has finally received the needed hint and persuasion to get the tree. Ten minutes after embarking on his journey, Daddy returns with a box. In it is an eight-foot pseudo-spruce with a lifetime guarantee. With guests mere moments from arriving, Mama pounds out the piecrust dough several extra times as Daddy undertakes assembly.

This Christmas scenario illustrates "good" will in two different ways. As we consider the Greek definition of "good" as being "beneficial," the artificial tree is beneficial, because it is better than having no tree at all. And, Daddy wants you to remember that it's the thought that counts, right?

We may also see this as "good" will, because mama exercised such in restraining herself from using her rolling pin on Daddy's person.

Another way to describe this "good" will of God is as "good enough." Many too many people have settled for "good enough" when it comes to choices of mates or living life, in general. Yes, it may be true that having a spouse is "beneficial" in that each is no longer alone, but one may find out very soon that not being alone is no cure-all for loneliness. (See Proverbs 21:19 for the sage wisdom of Solomon, a man with much marriage experience.)

Now let's reboot our Christmas tree story and see what happens when Mama and Daddy are a little more clued-in with each other and the next level of God's will.

God's "Acceptable" Will

Christmas week arrives and Daddy, without hint or persuasion, embarks on his annual tree-hunting journey. He returns with a good tree. It will take a bit of work to get it to fit in the stand and a little more work to get it to fit into it's place in the living room. After Mama hides the thin spots with tinsel and hangs the final ornaments, she steps back to admire her creation.

Well done, both Mama and Daddy - very acceptable scenario on all fronts.

The Greek definition of "acceptable" is "well-pleasing." Not only was Mama pleased that Daddy did his job without provocation, but she was also pleased that the good tree became a great tree when she set her hands to it.

One more reboot. If you've ever dreamed of a perfect Christmas holiday, it may have gone something like this:

God's "Perfect" Will

Daddy assures mama that he has everything Christmas tree under control this year. She is a little nervous, but trusts her husband. He rarely lets her down.

Christmas week arrives and with it a knock on the door. The entire extended family yells "surprise!" – children, grandchildren, nieces, nephews, brothers, sisters, etc. (They're all staying in hotels, but will hang at Mama's house for all the good stuff). With them, they brought the tree, which was pre-measured and fitted into its stand. Along with the tree are coolers full of food, cooking utensils and baking paraphernalia. Uncle Bud even brought a deep fryer for a turkey experiment he's wanted to try. Mama is led into the living room to visit, while the rest of the family begins decorating, cooking and baking – a process that will continue unabated for several days of Christmas bliss.

See, I told you it was perfect – well worth the wait and the trust.

The Greek definition of "perfect" is "complete." What could be more complete than mama's instant Christmas memory? There is power and satisfaction in waiting for His perfection.

"Mate" – as from Isaiah 34:16 KJV

Hebrew 7468, **reʾûwth**, *reh-ooth'; a female associate, gen. an additional one, another, neighbor*

PART TWO

Focus on the person, not the need

5

The Identity

Break the smoky mirror

Personal testimony

I accepted Jesus as my personal Savior when I was nine years old. The organist played "Just As I Am" at the altar call for the second week in a row. I felt a tugging on my heart as I walked the aisle and faced the pastor. I remember turning around long enough to see my mother and her mother scrambling for tissues as my little brother looked on in wide-eyed wonder. I was baptized a few weeks later in April 1973.

My childhood years were full of Scouts and baseball. I dutifully went to Sunday school and church until neither held my interest. At age 17, my high school experience endowed me with every bit of knowledge that a guy needed to know to succeed in life. I was saved when I was a kid, so I had my ticket to heaven. Now, it was time to do what I wanted…at least that's what I thought.

I discovered music, joined a band and began dating. What I didn't realize was that I was also forming my own brand of religion. It could probably best be described as Justification-ism. Therefore, I became a "justification-ist."

As you will see in my example, as I did, Justification-ism tests God's grace. It raises a smoky mirror. Break the mirror! Gaze instead into the perfection of Jesus' face.

Justificationism

I justified sleeping with my girlfriend "because we loved each other." I justified not going to church because I played music on Saturday nights until really late. The fluctuating tenets of Justification-ism were freeing. I was free from all guilt and condemnation that the 10 Commandments wrought. But, deep down, I knew that none of the tenets of this personalized feel-good theology were especially fulfilling.

I was very driven to succeed, but also a pragmatist. My passion was music, so I put everything into my band, saving just enough to pass my college business classes in case the band thing went bust.

The band thing did go bust and, at age 22, I moved to Music City USA. I enrolled in a Music Business program – one of only a handful of such programs in the country. The program just happened to be offered by a Baptist College. I remember praying for God to bless my decision - one of only a handful of prayers that I ever remember praying. It also exemplified who was in charge of my life. I certainly didn't ask Him if He wanted me to move, I just did it and asked Him to bless it. <Told ya I already knew everything...>

He actually did bless it! I found a great job working in a record store. I worked there 40 hours a week while taking a full class load with as many internships as I could cram into my schedule. I put my performing career on the back burner after my first Nashville audition. It was the first audition I didn't pass. The competition in Music City proved to be much tougher than back home.

My dad, a life-long musician, introduced me to his friend, who ran a record label. I was soon interning for his recording studio as an engineer. I left that pursuit when I failed my second audition. Making the piano player replay his part because the intern accidentally recorded over it, I found, is not conducive to employment hitherto.

But, I did finally land a job in the music business. My dad's friend, the label head, hired me into his sales and marketing department. All of those back-up business classes paid off and I nearly broke my arm patting myself on the back.

It was during my time at the record label that I met a girl I'll call Theresa. She was a street-wise beauty who worked for one of my company's vendors. We began dating and I, in effect, moved in with her. Although I kept my own apartment, I spent very little time there, rarely needing to wash my sheets.

My religion of Justification overlaid nicely with my circumstances. I was on a successful track in the music business and was living with a girl who satisfied my desire for companionship. I began to convince myself that I was living the American dream and deserved the happiness I was receiving. I even remember saying out loud to Theresa and her tween-aged daughter as we drove around looking for a house together, "You know what? I am happy."

It tasted like an old shoe in my mouth as soon as I said it. After quizzical looks from both girls, it was never mentioned again.

6

The Numbers

100 million Elvis fans can't be wrong

<u>Terminology needs updating</u>

So, how many need to be *Singled In*, anyway? Let's look at the potential need pool. Many unmarried Americans don't even identify themselves as "single." Because they are parents, have partners or are widowed, they use other terms to describe themselves, like "single again" or simply "unmarried."

So, if the need pool doesn't consider itself to be single, then it becomes a difficult task to find help. The social nets of the church and civic groups must make it a priority then to make themselves known to the searching need pool.

<u>US census numbers</u>

So how many people are currently in this need pool? According to the 2010 US Census, there were 99.6 M unmarried adults (18 and older) in America, up from 89.8M in 2005. Let's see, if the total US population is 300 M and 100 M are unmarried, that means there is an astounding 1/3 of us who are in need of being *Singled In*!

Here are some more numbers to show the need. It's OK if your eyes glaze over a little during this section. This book will remain on your shelf as a reference, so feel free to grow a little glassy-eyed now, but keep this book handy for when the big questions arise, like...

When your group leader asks you, "Exactly what percentage of US residents are actually not married?" You can grab this handy manual and tell him/her, "There are 43.6% of all US adults who are unmarried, which is up from 41% in 2005, my dear leader person."

You can then boggle an usher's mind by quoting the fact that 61% of unmarried US residents have never been married with another 23.8% being divorced and 14.4% widowed.

Other important demographic considerations include the 16.4 M of unmarried US residents 65 and older (14.9M in 2005) comprise 16.5% (14% in 2005) of all single adults.

...and, that 59.1 M (55M in 2005) households are maintained by unmarried men or women, which is 45% of all US households

Along with 31.4 M (29.9M in 2005) people who live alone. That's 27% (26% in 2005, 17% in 1970) of all US households.

Dating Services

A final statistic to illustrate a need for a new approach to singles ministry is the fact that there are 393 US dating services as of 2007 (including internet services). These companies employed 3125 (4300 in 2002) and generated $928M ($489M in 2002) in revenue. One can conclude that although the total number of companies shrank from 904 in 2002, the amount of revenue generated nearly doubled. The market seems to have shaken out all but the most successful services, while increasing revenues to a growing population of users in just a short 5-year span.

OK, in simple math terms, 100M + 43.6% + 61% + 16.4M + 59.1M + 31.4M + $928M = A WHOLE LOT OF ALONE-NESS! Parse these numbers any way you wish, but they all equal a huge, growing and exceedingly diverse need.

7

The New Identity

Wait...what?!

When you meet God's Holy Spirit and ask Him to change you, expect drama. Justificationism allowed me to build my life however I wanted. What I didn't notice is that this juvenile creation of mine was not real balanced. To those who knew me, it looked like a game of Jenga® poised for the next breath-holding move.[9]

<u>Balcony story</u>

One thing Theresa liked to do was go to church on Saturday nights. She liked the upbeat music and the upbeat message from the young pastor. Her brand of Justification-ism allowed her to do what she wanted during the week as long as she confessed sometime on the weekend. As for me, I quit going to church as a teenager and felt that my weekly Baptist chapel service at college would keep God happy.

She invited me to go to church with her, and, after a few declinations, I eventually did. We compromised, though, and went to one of the church's Sunday morning services. We backslid Baptist-slash-Justification-ists need to have at least a modicum of a comfort zone.

Holy Cow! The place was packed to the brim – probably 1000 people! We searched for a seat and I started seeing famous people in the crowd. We finally squeezed into a pew and the music started. It was not my Southern Baptist organ music. Everyone stood, clapped, cheered; danced, shouted...I was scared to death.

Many weeks later and after she convinced me that Saturday nights were more subdued, we entered the sanctuary again. This time we sat in the balcony. It was just Theresa, her daughter and I.

The band began to play a modern worship chorus. The pastor stood to the side of the band with his eyes closed praising and singing to God. He would sing a little, then mumble a little, all the time swaying from side to side. He kept the microphone in his hand in case someone left car lights on, I guessed.

The first song subsided and the next began. The pastor pressed the microphone to his mouth and shouted praises to The Almighty as the musicians continued to play.

Then suddenly, the pastor broke into the song. This time it wasn't to sing along or interject praise. He actually told the band "Stop the music! Stop the music!"

I had witnessed many oddities at this church already, so I just put this one into my back pocket with the others. It wouldn't stay back there for long, though.

"Please, stop the music," the pastor continued. "The Lord has given me a word and it is <u>strong</u>."

Again, I was intrigued, but incapable, I thought, of surprise. I was thinking "OK, I've seen this kind of thing on TV before. I wonder which schmuck he's going to try to con."

"The Lord has given me a name. It's the name of someone here tonight. That name is Jeff. Jeff... Brother... The Lord Jesus is calling you back home. He is jealous for you and wants you back."

He motioned to the bandleader and the song began anew.

This backslid-Baptist boy was more than a little overwhelmed. I heard my first and last names spoken by someone who didn't know me or have any idea that I was in attendance that night. I thought to myself, "He's talking about me!" I even looked over at Theresa and said that very thing out loud. She seemed to know that God had entered the picture and our life together would never be the same. She sat next to me in the pew shaking her head, afraid to look me in the eye.

More Lord

Theresa was right. Our life together changed. I began going to services regularly. I began learning the praise songs and even singing them to myself during the week. Wednesday nights were teaching times. I started reading the Bible to keep up with the history lessons that even had practical contemporary application. I had swallowed God's hook.

I wanted to please Him. I wanted my life to be free from anything that kept me from the energy I felt when I worshipped Him and was around others who did the same.

So, I gathered my courage and confronted Theresa. Sheepishly I told her that I believed that our living together outside of marriage was wrong. "God has something better for us," I said with not much conviction. It may not have been the most powerful first step ever taken, but it was a first step nonetheless.

I don't remember her reply. There may not have been one. Part of her comfortable world of indulgences was ending and she didn't want to discuss it. I was not much better. I knew that I wanted to live for God, but I didn't want to change much to accomplish it. I had confronted the situation and that was "good enough." My old religion of Justification-ism kicked back in and it gave me the excuse to relax. My thinking shaped by this self-made religion convinced me that I had made a huge step with the confrontation. All I needed do in the meantime was wait and flow with any changes. Until then, living the same life would be OK.

What I hadn't counted on was that God was going to deal with my terrestrial justification thinking at the same time He would deal with my lifestyle and relationships.

Ch-ch-ch-changes

Time passed and I was enjoying this new church thing. I started making some casual friends, but always at a safe, and I thought, controllable, distance.

My relationship with Theresa was strained, as I could not find a way to reconcile our situation with God's preferred behavior. Finally, I came to the realization that she was not going to change her attitude and that if I wanted change, it would need to come from me.

The internal stress of those days was intense. My heart and brain swirled in two separate directions, intersecting at my soul. I prayed, I cried, I prayed, I yelled...my poor steering wheel certainly has some tales to tell.

One morning, as I left her place to go to mine for the day's work readiness, I was praying, crying and banging my fists on the steering wheel, "Lord, just get me out of this situation. I can't stand it anymore. I want out!"

As plain as Miss Muffett's cottage cheese I heard Him say, "Ask her to marry you."

Wait...what?

I instantly stopped crying, blinked repeatedly, wiped my eyes and said correctively, "I said I wanted out."

He repeated, "Ask her to marry you."

Wow! OK. Let's review…boy wants freedom. Boy literally cries out for God to give him freedom. God says, "Get married." That about sums it up.

As you can imagine, I grappled with this exchange for quite a while. I began pricing new steering wheels.

Eventually though, I began to see the wisdom. God was going to change Theresa. She would probably repent of our sinful lifestyle and go straight arrow. He would purify us and we would both wear white on our wedding day. Yup, that's what would happen.

Lord have mercy on old dogs, young children and idiots named Jeffrey Lee Brothers.

On a mission

I'm a planner, so the next few weeks were exciting for me. I shopped for a ring, picked out the perfect restaurant and hired a horse-drawn carriage for the proposal. I even made a background music tape of our favorite romantic songs to play in the car on the way to the restaurant to set the mood. If I were going to do this, I would do it right.

The night was perfect - so, too, the restaurant. So perfect, in fact, I nearly popped the question inside. A nervous energy began to present itself as I began feeling my whole body tremble with anticipation.

After dinner, we walked toward the valet stand, but instead of our car, we stepped into the waiting carriage. The driver's stovepipe hat and the rhythmic clip clopping of the horse's hooves on Nashville cobblestone evoked a simpler, less troubling time. The warm air did little to soothe the nerves, though, and I continued to experience intermittent tremors.

We found ourselves pausing in our romantic conversation to listen to the horse amble. It was during one such dramatic pause that I found the courage to ask, "Will you marry me?"

With the exuberance of a belated birthday wish she mumbled, "I don't know what to say."

And with that, my last candle was extinguished.

Crest-fallen I think I managed to say something like, "Don't say anything right now. We'll talk about it later."

We never did.

My ego smashed. My plans ruined. I ducked my head and quit trying to make any sense of anything. I gave up. I was too emotionally weak to change anything, so I dutifully kept to my routines.

Nine months passed.

One Sunday morning, an issue arose with her daughter. It was a recurring innocuous, annoying thing that I was powerless to change. But, for some reason, it struck me the wrong way this time – as in, "I want no more of this" kinda wrong. In the past, I swallowed this feeling like cod liver oil, but today, Super Bowl® Sunday, I felt empowered to keep my feelings where I could get at them if I needed them.[10]

During the previous year's Super Bowl®, Theresa feigned illness or hangover or something and I wound up watching the game on a 15" TV with the sound turned down so she could sleep. She had a controlling tendency to marginalize things that I enjoyed. Forcing me to watch football in such a manner re-established her alpha female position in our relationship.

As this Super Bowl® Sunday began to unfold, I could tell that my opportunity to watch the game on a suitable screen with suitable sound was fading. I don't remember the details, but I do remember the frustration and anger that arose within me as trivial circumstances lent to plan changes.

The last of many of those plan changes sent Theresa and her daughter out of the house on some sort of errand for a friend. Something inside me, whether it was my pent up anger, my need for change, my desire to see the Super Bowl® on a big TV, the Holy Spirit or a combination, led me to leave Theresa's house, go to my apartment, order a pizza and watch the game all by myself. So, I did.

<u>A New Beginning</u>

The next morning, after spending the night at my own apartment, all of the things that I had stockpiled at her house during our 4-year relationship were in a heap in my front yard.

The site was magnificent! A pile of junk grotesquely symbolizing several things simultaneously – my proposal, my relationship, my feelings, and my life…I couldn't have asked for a better ending. I was finished with her, finished with the relationship and finally, good with God. The relief was palpable and welcome.

He knew exactly how she would react to my marriage proposal. Even though it took some time to gather my nerve, I was obedient to His specific instruction (proposal) and obedient to the man He called me to be (leaving).

I embraced that freedom I pounded the steering wheel in search of. Through the drama of a relationship that pounded the flesh out of me, I found my identity in Jesus. I saw a much stronger man in the mirror now. After He wiped the fog, there was less of me and more of Him in that facial reflection.

He got my attention by messing with my head that Saturday night the pastor stopped the music. It wasn't long after that He had my heart and devotion. Now, with this freedom, He wanted my face to look like His son. The only way to accomplish this is from the inside out.

As I continue to identify with Jesus, my character will shine forth through my demeanor. I will literally begin to look more and more like Jesus. "...a man's wisdom maketh his face to shine, and the hardness of his face shall be changed."[11]

Anyone who longs for real, tangible life with meaning and purpose must courageously pray, "More, Lord."

8

The Longing

Loneliness is a call to action

We humans were designed and built to be dependant beings. We are dependant upon God and each other. God is our fulfillment.[12] "I am the vine, ye are the branches: He that abideth in me, and I in him, the same beareth much fruit: for apart from me ye can do nothing."[13]

If we have a need, He will fill it. How He fills it is where the fun...excuse me, I meant where "others" come in. Did I say, "...where the FUN comes in?" Silly me. But, now that I mention it, I do have a fun little story to tell you that relates to our topic of belonging. Give me a sec to set it up for you.

Have you ever felt lonely? I know, that's like asking a pizza delivery guy if he'd like a bigger tip. Of course, we've all had those feelings of loneliness from time to time. These feelings are not exclusive to single people, though. Married folks, young, elderly and even very socially active people will deal with these feelings to varying degrees. So, don't think they will all magically go away once you get married or join a social group. Making a lasting relationship is certainly a great step in the right direction. That alone can dramatically diminish loneliness, by God's design. But, even those with an embarrassment of close, strong relationships will want something more.

<u>Prayer</u>

In times like those, the best thing to do is talk to God. He always wants to be with you and me. Quite often, He will give me instructions and directions on how and for whom to pray. I call it praying under the influence.

Sometimes I feel something like a mild depression. It's as if my gut (inner most being) is drawing me down to my knees. Early on, before I realized what was happening was a God thing, I would hold onto these burdens for hours, days, even weeks. The burden would eventually manifest itself into a real, mild depression. My body's reaction would be one of frustration and anger. I would attempt to relieve my worried soul by doing something outwardly physical.

Driving around until I calmed down worked sometimes. Hitting balls at the batting cage worked, too.

Eventually, I came to realize that this mild depression that I would feel was nothing more than a call to prayer by God Himself. So, like I was told to do in Sunday school, I have finally learned to cast my burden upon Him, who is able to take it away.

Now, when I feel such a burden, as soon as I can, I find a place to open up and let all of that burden release up from my gut, into my mouth, off my tongue and into His Kingdom.

I see this as one of my main purposes on earth. Whether I ever meet them or not, I am interceding for someone before the Almighty God. I pray until I feel the burden lift. Any loneliness or self-pity has been washed away in a swell of Spirit prayer. By connecting with God in prayer and interceding for someone else, He has replaced lonely feelings with purpose and people.

God Uses Loneliness

He also uses loneliness for His own purposes - as a mechanism to woo us unto Himself. Several times in scripture, He is described as and even calls Himself a jealous God. Through these lonely feelings He says, "I love you. I want to be with you. Let Me fill you. In Me is everything that you need. If you will wait for Me, you will begin to feel content again." This feeling of contentment is not in itself equal to being fulfilled, but, as you will see in the next chapter, it is a strong precursor.

Unfortunately, instead of filling ourselves with God, we have the means and ability to fill ourselves with things of this world. A short-lived and shallow contentment is the result.

Have you ever tried to brighten your mood with things like ice cream? Loud music? TV? Nail polish? Porn? New shoes? Sex? Travel? I would venture to say that most of us have tried a few things on this list. These things of the world were <u>designed</u> to make us feel better. And, in the right circumstance may even have a place in our lives. But, the trap is that too often, the low-hanging fruit of the world's trees is very tempting. We can easily fill ourselves with it, burn through it and fill ourselves again without ever acknowledging the Maker of it all. Repeat this cycle enough and it becomes a habit. Relent to the habit enough and it becomes an addiction for, which you will eventually need a "fix."

<u>The First Family</u>

This want of ours to belong or be special to someone has been around a long time. In the Garden of Eden, God created a natural outlet for Adam's feelings of being less than complete. Actually, if you look in Gen 2:20, God ran every kind of living land-based creature in front of Adam, to see which would satisfy his need for a companion. Adam named them all, but he never named one "wife" or "mate." So, God showed His love for Adam by fulfilling his needs in the person of Eve. He took a part of Adam's own body and customized the perfect fit for his natural needs.

God said during the creation of Eve, "...not good that the man should be alone."[14] By giving Eve unto Adam as his teammate, God gave us the model for marriage. However, God did not say, "...not good that EVERY man should be alone," or "every man shall have unto himself a help mate for life." Arguably, at this point in history, God had planned for the man and the woman to live in the Garden forever. He hadn't mentioned the rest of us yet (save for Moses' commentary in Gen 2:24). So, even though it's "not good" for Adam to be alone in the Garden, it can be perfectly fine for you or I to be unmarried in America. Don't worry. We're not really alone anyway. We're still part of God's plan. He has a magnificent way of including everyone that He creates into His plan. He's good like that.

Mates/spouses are God's model for filling our natural needs for intimate companionship. But, remember, He is a jealous God. His one-on-one relationship with you is more important to Him than even meeting your needs. Not only is He your Provider, He is your Provision. Unless or until He provides you with an earthly mate, He is your mate. We'll be talking about this concept more in Chapter 15.

Yes, a spouse/mate is a "good" thing and worthy of pursuit, but only if this pursuit is initiated or ordained (okayed) by God. In other words, "Seek ye first the Kingdom of God and his righteousness and all these things shall be added unto you."[15]

The First Church

God loves people. Through the sacrifice of Jesus, He gave Himself the pathway to be with you forever. And, forever doesn't begin when you die; it begins when you receive Him into your life here on earth. He will not only take up residence in your heart, He will interact with you in many ways, including and most importantly, other people. God calls us His body. Through us He is able to dress a wound, to kiss a face, to rally support, to encourage greatness and to dry eyes.

God wants to have a life with us. He will use the people in our lives to accomplish His goal. This also gives us the opportunity to meet God in a new way with each person we meet.

Have you ever prayed for something and wondered why you never saw the answer? Next time after you pray, notice the people in your life. God is good at using them to fulfill your earthly needs. And, He seems to like a little dramatic spice, too.

That brings us to that story I wanted to share. You'll see how God used a bunch of people to meet the emotional need of belonging for just one person. He pulled out all the stops and allowed us all to have some of that fun mentioned earlier, too.

Bachelor Auction Story

This story begins with my old buddy…let's call him…Barry. (That's what his mother called him, too. I'm not real concerned about his anonymity.) Several years ago, I had known Barry long enough for him to know that I loved kids. I'm not quite sure of his motivations for the event that I am about to tell. Perhaps they were conjoined to the point where helping abused children while simultaneously embarrassing me seemed perfectly natural to him. So be it.

The telephone conversation went something like this:

"Hey, Jeff"

"Yeah, buddy. What's up"?

"I'm involved with this charity that helps sexually abused children. Wanna help?"

"Sure! What do you need me to do?"

It was exactly two seconds after I uttered the line above that I wished I could un-utter it.

"I'm glad you asked! They are putting together a benefit bachelor auction and would love to have you in it."

<Silence>

"You'll love it"

<Silence>

"Hello?"

"I hate it"

"C'mon!"

Barry also knew me well enough to know that once I agreed to something, I would follow through. I was upset with myself for allowing my friendship to lower my guard and agree to an open-ended contract. They taught me better in business school...

After the initial shock wave subsided and allowed my brain to function in a reasoning capacity, I countered:

"OK. I said I would do it and I will. But, you gotta give me something."

"What's that?"

"I want time to perform a worship song."

"Done"

So, the night came and I arrived at the hotel in my tux with guitar in hand. I happened to know the MC of the event and spent as much time as I could talking with her so that I wouldn't be tempted to crack Barry over the head with my beautiful guitar. I loved that guitar.

So, I flitted between single women (and some who claimed to be single, but whose true situation is still unknown). The goal was to "sell" the date package that I was asked to put together. In so doing, ladies would anticipate a glorious future date and bid accordingly when I glimmered onto the stage. The auction was being held in Southern Illinois, 200 miles from my home in Nashville. So, it wasn't difficult to create a mystical travel date event with a Music City backdrop.

The time arrived. We 30 bachelors took our places backstage. Soon, we heard the disco music pump up to 10 and gleeful war hoops from the estrogen and alcohol-enriched crowd.

One by one we marched, danced, pranced, fell out onto the stage. Each of us received our cursory introduction and then the bidding began.

"Who'll give me $50 for Dave and his backpacking trip to the Indian cave?"
"God, is this really happening?" I asked
"Go with it, Jeffrey. I got your back." God replied
"Easy for you to say," I thought, hoping it wasn't loud enough thought for Him to hear.

I was number 25 of 30. My time finally came. The disco music stopped, but that dratted disco ball kept right on twisting and glittering. I was introduced. I pulled up a stool and sang my worship song, preached a 30 second sermon and walked over to the "X" on the stage.

The disco music unapologetically thumped back up into my face and the bidding war began. Several hundred dollars later, this piece of meat returned to the cooler of my humiliation. (No, I was not the largest prize that night. I was second. Although, to be fair, that guy paid his secretary to prime the bidding to ensure his victory. So, you be the judge. And, thanks for asking).

After all us bachelors were purchased, it was time to meet our benefactors. I met my girl. We made small talk and discussed her trip to Nashville for our date. We exchanged telephone numbers and the affair found its end.

A month went by and the auction-date arrived and along with it, my date, Sarah (her true identity I WILL keep anonymous.)

We lunched at Planet Hollywood and took a brief walking tour of Broadway then a break to check her into her hotel room. Later, I picked her up for dinner at Opryland and a night at the Grand Ole Opry. We would see Loretta Lynn, her favorite perform.

After our date, I pulled into the hotel parking lot. During our time that day, we talked about many things, including Jesus. He would come up in conversation as casual as you please. While we sat in the parking lot, I asked Sarah if she would like to know Jesus personally. She did. We prayed. She does.

So, the lesson is that when you put Him up front, He'll get your back, even if you end up looking like a sideshow. It was worth all the effort and humiliation to gain a sister that day.

God fulfilled her longing to belong in a big, dramatic way. What a show He can put on when He feels so inclined!

Excuse me...what's that, Paul? Oh yes, the Apostle would like to add something here, too.

> *"But I would have you to be free from cares. He that is unmarried is careful for the things of the Lord, how he may please the Lord: but he that is married is careful for the things of the world, how he may please his wife, and is divided. So also the woman that is unmarried and the virgin is careful for the things of the Lord, that she may be holy both in body and in spirit: but she that is married is careful for the things of the world, how she may please her husband. And this I say for your own profit; not that I may cast a snare upon you, but for that which is seemly, and that ye may attend upon the Lord without distraction."*[16]

The bachelor auction may stretch the boundaries of the word "seemly" that Paul used above, but to introduce Sarah to Jesus in this way just would not have been possible as a married man.

Even with that said Paul's point about remaining unmarried is one well taken. We'll discuss it some more in Chapter 13.

It's easy to fill the emptiness within with the low-hanging fruit of the world. For real change, purpose and fulfillment, following God can be just the adventure you need.

Illustration by: Brian Frost

"...there is a friend that sticketh closer than a brother"

Proverbs 18:24b ASV

Verse refers to the closest mate you can have, Jesus.

PART THREE:

Discovering self by helping others

9

The Fulfillment

Everyone is created for something more

Everyone each day awakens with a connection to the earth. We live our lives as terrestrial beings. Multitudes of us, these same people, awaken with a yearning, even a longing for something more. It is not enough to live a life connected to just the mundane – the ground. We dream of a full life connected to a lofty purpose.

We figure that if we know what our purpose is, we need only live in that purpose and our need to feel fulfilled will be met. In other words, living a purposeful life + contentment = fulfillment.

Is this true? Can it be that simple, that all we need to do to be happy is to find and live our purpose?

As a matter of fact, "yes!"

Ooooo...audacious. Here's what I'm talking about.

Fulfillment vs. Feeling

First, fulfillment is not a feeling. It is much less fleeting. Fulfillment is a deep knowing that no matter where you are, what you are doing or how convoluted your path may currently be, you are part of greater purpose. It is a state of being dependant upon one's relationship to God. If you are "filled up" with God, you have allowed Him into the various places in your soul (mind, will, emotions). And, if you're filled up with God; Who is life, love and truth, it's a heck of a lot easier to flip the contentment switch on in your brain.

And, don't confuse fulfillment with contentment. To be content or "good with the world," you simply need to be in the correct frame of mind. We use all sorts of tricks to convince our brains to "turn our frowns upside down," don't we? Guys take to the woods, skip shaving or drive around rockin' the door panels off the car. And girls...girls have more of these tricks than I can possibly list. But, no matter one's gender, being content is simply a feeling. It's how you pursue that feeling, which will determine whether it will last or not.

A construction worker can draw great feelings of accomplishment when he sees the house he has built with his co-workers. He went to work every day for months buoyed by the expectation of good pay and this feeling of contentment.

A mother has the same expectation while raising her children. She works day after day to give her kids their best opportunities. One day, (and I dare say many in between) during a graduation or wedding ceremony, she will have an emotional payoff in a satisfying feeling of happiness or contentment.

Plateaus

By no means am I pointing to our construction worker or our mother as examples of bad things. These folks have worked hard and should enjoy their feelings. What I am saying is that these life plateaus, should not be looked upon as an end result or fulfillment. They are meaningful emotional plateaus, but, if you want lasting fulfillment, God has more.

Unfortunately, it is possible to build a life of plateaus and memories. Many hard-working people have built families, businesses, and fortunes, only to decide that this pattern of living from peak to peak is "good enough" – the good outweighs the bad. They have resigned themselves to remembering the happy feelings over and over. So, they declare themselves content.

So, really, this attempt at fulfillment is not fulfillment at all. They have convinced themselves that a patchwork of proud plateaus will keep them warm through life. Or, they have chosen to cap-off their souls and call them full. Either way, this safety zone of a manageable life minimizes fear, pain and hardship and acquiesces to a paltry modicum of fulfillment. And that's "good enough" for them.

I'll ask again, is there still something missing? Are you satisfied with "good enough?" Is there a gnawing or maybe, just a tingle that you have been denying or hiding for years that is telling you that there is something even more than the great things you can enjoy with your five senses?

In the previous chapter, we talked about how God did not create the things of this world for us to continually fill ourselves with them. Stuff of the world is temporal and made to meet temporal needs. None of it lasts. If we're not constantly on guard, we can fill up with this type of junk food and have no room for the Godly nourishment we really need. We take. We use. We take some more. This cycle is actually a counterfeit of the true process of fulfillment. God's process fills you up, gives you a place to pour out and then refills you.

Notice the subtle differences in God's process and the world's counterfeit. Both would have you fill yourself first. Both God and the world say, "Fill yourself with me." It's like choosing between a balanced breakfast or boxed cereal. The nutrition of God fills you to overflowing meeting not only your needs, but allowing you enough energy to help others. You can burn through two bowls of boxed cereal in half an hour.

So, the state of fulfillment is active. Fill up with God. Pour out to the people around you. Fill up with God again. Personally, I would rather my soul be filled, regularly – not just to some ambiguous plateau. I would rather my soul glass be running over with bubbly stuff than to be satisfied with half a glass of flat soda. And I certainly won't be trying to find some lid to put on it.

And, that elusive feeling of contentment that I mentioned earlier is a direct result of being fulfilled. A continuing feeling of contentment is a good sign that the process of being filled by God, pouring out and getting refilled is alive and working in you. "And to know the love of Christ, which passeth knowledge, that ye might be filled with all the fullness of God."[17] Purpose + contentment = fulfillment. This is Kingdom living.

10

The Purpose

No fulfillment without purpose

<u>MORE is better</u>

So, where is this mystic, never-ending two-liter bottle of bubbling soul stuff? It has a brand name. We'll call it MORE. MORE is an exponential experience relative to this terrestrial existence. MORE is the spiritual life that has been going on long before the temporal one was ever formed.

You may choose to believe that humans evolved from a primordial ooze of a fortunate concoction of elements over eons of time. That notion is one shared by many people. These folks also tend to believe in only a few measurable dimensions, too. For them, that explanation of life's origins is "good enough."

True Life is Science Fiction
=====

I choose to believe that there is a parallel universe, not unlike one Gene Roddenberry may have cooked up for a Star Trek® episode.[18] Each word spoken and action committed has implications, even repercussions in our twin universe. When we shout certain things, throngs of souls echo and join us. When we speak commands, winged creatures bolt into action. When we hurt, a healer instantly begins tending to our wounds. When we cry out to be saved from our hopeless life, a savior astride a white horse jumps at the opportunity to make all things new.

I choose to believe the words and stories of the greatest adventure novel I ever read. When I read it over and over again, I find myself in its pages. It's full of brave warriors, ugly giants, devastating catastrophes, winged creatures, chilling ghosts, greasy goblins, gigantic beasts and other weird phenomena.

I believe the Bible embodies many things. It is an accurate historical reference of people, places, and events; a map to hidden treasure on earth and in heaven; and a love story of God, His Son and human creation.

I have found my fulfillment and purpose in the person of Jesus. I identify with him. It is the most challenging and rewarding life I could have chosen. It is a marriage of the terrestrial/temporal and the spiritual. My purpose is to glorify the God who made it all for me and to tell those who haven't discovered the entirety of this full life all about it. Married or not, this is every single person's fulfilling purpose.

<u>Feed My Sheep</u>

"How does God want me to glorify Him?" "What does my purpose looks like?" These questions can only be answered by The Almighty. The answers, though, I can guarantee will involve other people. God will inevitably use the *Singled In* concept to make sure that you are fulfilled and that He is glorified.

A good first step toward this fulfillment is to attend a church. Don't glaze over that last sentence. Don't just go to a church building and sit in silence. With that attitude, you will undoubtedly feel lonelier than before you went in. "Attend" is an action verb. To attend is to show attention, interact with others.

Step 1: Get up.

Step 2: Go some place where a vibrant church body meets.

Step 3: Interact with church members – a.k.a. getting *Singled In*!

As you connect with others, you will be a recipient of the love of Jesus <u>and</u>, if you hang around long enough, you will learn how to dish it out, too. "Feed my sheep," He told Peter.[19]

Like most of us, you may first identify with the sheep. We all need to be fed and attended. Eventually, The Good Shepherd will teach you, too, how to feed His sheep.

11

The Challenge

Life is hard

There is not a perfect church body or civic group on earth. All are led by sinful humans redeemed by Jesus. People hurt each other regularly. Through our pain and weakness, God's power is perfected as He is glorified.

<u>Judas Is Scary, Yes?</u>

A few months after my dramatic encounter with God and the subsequent separation from Theresa I told you about in Chapter 7, I met Frank. He was a friend of a friend and the three of us began having lunches together. We quickly became three musketeers. No, better make that, three stooges. We all had at least a perfunctory history in radio. That fact alone may give you an idea of our collective sense of humor.

Eventually, my co-worker left the company and lunches with Frank weren't as plentiful. Many months passed until he invited me to join in some functions with his church's singles group.

I went with him and his group to events like bowling, movies, dining out, etc. It wasn't long before I was attending the prayer/ministry meetings. I enjoyed the activities and the people.

Frank's church was large enough to successfully institute the *Singled Out* approach to Singles ministry that we discussed in Chapter 1. The church had several different classes based not only by age, but also by interest. If a single person wasn't happy with his/her group's activities, he/she could simply bounce to one of the other groups.

For the most part, this approach seemed to work well. However, this ability to bounce could enable "action" seekers to survey the entire field.

I began noticing that more girls than guys were showing up at Frank's meetings. As a single guy interested in finding a good church-going Christian gal of his own, I conscientiously ignored this self-serving dynamic and its repercussions at the time.

It was at a New Year's party that I met a particularly attractive and interesting church-going gal. Frank had been chatting each of us up to the other as matchmaker, so when I officially met her, we had a little back-story to discuss.

We started seeing each other outside of the singles group and I started having real feelings for her. Of course, she was one of the main topics of lunch conversation between Frank and I. As my feeling for her deepened, I began to sense a weird resistance in my friend. In my naïveté, I didn't think much of it. I would think much more about it in due time, though.

Eventually, I was approached by one of the other female group members, who revealed some startling personal knowledge. Our leader, my friend Frank, was much closer with some of the female members than this type of parochial relationship should warrant. He had surveyed the "action" and, as leader, several times carved a path for it to his bedroom door.

It's certainly not the first time a trusted leader has taken advantage of the responsibility with, which he was entrusted. But, it was the first time that I had a personal stake in such a situation. I was devastated – betrayed by two very close friends. What hurt me most, though, were not the betrayals. It was that he was abusing his leadership role. I didn't have a place in my brain anywhere that could explain how someone could have trampled so flippantly upon the fragile hearts who trusted him to exemplify the love of Jesus.

Dr. Billy Graham made it a policy from the beginning of his ministry, never to meet with someone of the opposite gender behind closed doors. If it were necessary to meet with a woman, he would have a female member of his ministry team in the room, too. At the very least, he would keep the door open so others could see that there was nothing untoward happening and the woman would feel the safety of an easy exit. Dr. Graham planted this above-reproach standard firmly in the ground for all to see. It shows a deep respect of God and His children. I challenge us all to follow his lead. Had it been followed, the chapter you are reading now would never have been written.

<u>Jesus Applied</u>

I gathered some of the singles group together for a strategy meeting and studied Matthew 18:15-17 ASV:

> *And if thy brother sin against thee, go, show him his fault between thee and him alone: if he hear thee, thou hast gained thy brother. But if he hear thee not, take with thee one or two more, that at the mouth of two witnesses or three every word may be established. And if he refuse to hear them, tell it unto*

> *the church: and if he refuse to hear the church also, let him be unto thee as the Gentile and the publican.*

I approached Frank with Jesus' action plan and asked him to repent. He did not. Weeks passed. I approached him again, this time as a member of a group of three. No repentance. Weeks passed. Finally, as directed by scripture, the three of us gathered others affected by his actions and approached the church leadership. Frank was asked to step down from his leadership post. I lost both a close friend and potential mate through the process.

Glorified

It takes a little contemplation to see where God is glorified in my betrayal story. To the best of my knowledge, Frank remains unrepentant. However, many of the others involved in this situation have allowed God to catch their fall and raise them up to new heights. He allowed me to exercise some maturity and follow His Matthew 18 outline of confrontation to a successful end. Now, I am able to give you the report of

God's goodness in a bad situation. That's how God is glorified – in our drama and our mundane. He has a plan to prosper us that includes a hopeful future of fulfillment and purpose.[20]

"Good on ya, **mate***"*
Australian saying

Meaning, "Good job, my friend"

PART FOUR:

"Singleness" is an opportunity

12

The Implementation

Positively influence your community

A *Singled In* vision is a rounded approach, which involves unmarrieds of all ages in community, where the focus is less on dating and more on living and giving.

It is also one of inclusion. Singles-only events or social mixers have their place and can be extremely effective as outreach tools. But, if you are an unmarried person already participating in your local community, these types of events should not be the main point of contact or interaction. Needs and growth can be missed.

<u>Simple act of service</u>

So, I can hear you asking, "but breaking singles into groups and having singles-only events is the only way we've ever done it." And some others are saying, "Our town is so small, we don't have anything for singles to do." OK, let's look at what I mean by implementing a *Singled In* approach.

Singled In does not require a full-time leader for the idea to be implemented. Remember, it is a mindset. Once you get the main concept, then you'll be able to put some structure to it and even build a system, if that is what is needed. Here, the idea is for unmarried folks to interact with others, regardless of marital status, and then one single person with the vision can implement it.

I mean every family at some point, needs a babysitter; a person to mow the lawn; a person to run errands or do odd jobs. Offer yourself as a willing participant to a family. "Hey guys, if you need your lawn mowed, I'm available." You have just *Singled* yourself *In*! Simple as that.

Does your church or civic group already have a dedicated ministry to its unmarried members? Great! These ideas in this book can be folded right into the existing structure.

Let's say your singles group is getting together for a movie night. Why not suggest a little change this week? See if the group would consider going to an age-appropriate movie for kids. Then, include some children from your community. Their parents might enjoy the break and you, dear reader, will have exercised the *Singled In* vision and advanced it to both family generations.

"We have a singles group, I think. But, it's kinda in name-only." Then what it may need is an infusion of fresh ideas – like *Singled In*!

Point Person

You see the need, but no one seems to want to lead the crusade? Then, allow me to suggest that you, dear reader, may be the one to jump in. You don't need to be unmarried to care for and serve unmarried people. After all, you can certainly relate to many of their situations - being a veteran of singleness yourself.

Once you have taken the initiative and contacted your community leaders with this great new idea you have for singles, you can take all of the credit when it works expectantly well. After your leaders agree that there is a need and that your passion for the work makes you the perfect point person, it's time to start saving the world.

In some way, you need to be introduced as the point person of the *Singled In* movement. Offer to wash your pastor's car in exchange for 5 minutes at a weekend service to introduce yourself to your congregation and cast the vision. Make sure to talk about your first implementation event to excite your fans.

You may not be comfortable making announcements to large groups of people. That's OK. Public speaking is not a pre-requisite. All you really need to propagate the vision is willingness. You may ask your pastor or an elder to champion you and your cause.

"Folks, this *Singled In* idea that Pat has is a breath of fresh air. Now, you married people, don't zone out on me here. This affects you as much as it does any unmarried person. Check your bulletin for the place and time of the first meeting."

Social networking is a great way to kick off a *Singled In* event or meeting. Start a forum, a group or chat room online. Even if you are the only person who shows up for an advertised event or meeting, tell the cyber world how much better it will be to have them involved. Cast that vision and do not despise small beginnings.[21]

In my case, my pastors gave me the pulpit one Valentine's Sunday morning. I had nearly an hour to teach my local church body about being *Singled In*. They and our eldership got behind the idea that day in 2010 and have encouraged it ever since.

I can almost hear your creative juices flowing as you are reading this, so it's certain that you need no help in coming up with great ideas to get going with this game-changing *Singled In* thing. So, since you're busily working on your ideas right now, let me share some more of mine with the other readers.

Idea 0

Most of my experiences have been in church setting, but *Singled In* will work anywhere. Whether you're thinking of implementing it into a religious, civic or other benevolence group, knowing with whom you will be working and serving is a foundational step. You need to meet your people.

If there is already an active singles group, make a vocal announcement, bulletin board message, social network, email, text blast – whatever works best to gather this group together. Frankly, starting a mouth-to-mouth campaign works fairly well, too. Food is usually a good incentive.

"Hey Billy, Jeffrey is getting a group together for lunch. He said to get as many as we can and meet in the parking lot."

Or, you could try a slightly more sneaky approach and disguise your invitation as a wicked rumor.

"Suzie, I'm not sure what's going on, but Jeffrey wants to tell us all something big. It sounded to me like a confession of some kind. Juicy!"

If you're starting *Singled In* from scratch and don't already have a singles group, you won't have the luxury of pinpointing your announcement. But, I already know that you are a creative visionary. You're reading this book! So, a person with your skills can figure out a way to spread the word through your community, if none of my suggestions do the trick.

After you've got your group together, you can briefly share the *Singled In* concept. Those interested in finding out more should meet you for a more detailed meeting where the group will gather ideas and gauge a participation quotient. Don't forget names, numbers, emails, etc., and contact information of any absentees.

Idea 1

For *Singled In* to thrive in a church setting, it's important that leadership understands the concept. For a glimpse at a church leader who doesn't quite get that concept, see Brother Bill's Bungle in Chapter 1.

Why not set a short meeting with your leaders and cast the vision? Your married pastors, elders, deacons, etc. can be its best promoters.

In my church, we don't take communion without the pastor insisting that all single persons find a family with whom to break the Lord's bread.

Our married leaders tend to seek out singles and invite them to sit with their families during service. They make it a habit to invite them to lunch or to hang out and have fun in their homes.

These married folks are implementing the *Singled In* approach.

Idea 2

Since you'll be washing your pastor's car already anyway after you were given five minutes behind the podium last weekend, why not put together a whole car washing service to the single moms in your assembly? This will give you a chance to meet the single moms and find out their other needs.

As point person you can publicly guarantee that several unmarried folks will be washing cars. And, just as importantly, solicit the participation of some married folks and their children in the event. Make a public challenge. Do what you need to do putting married and unmarried folks together working for the cause of clean cars.

Idea 3

Meeting occasionally with the most enthusiastic *Singled In* warriors (married or unmarried) in your assembly is always a good way to stay connected. It's necessary to keep the message fresh and the service relevant.

Whether begun as a concerted effort within church walls or a simple act of service in the community, the *Singled In* mindset will reveal opportunities to serve and grow.

13

The Illusion

Is marriage an illusion?

<u>Godly disillusionment</u>

Not all single people will marry or re-marry. At some point you knew we would discuss marriage. Why is that? You read the table of contents, didn't you? Clever. Well, we've talked a lot about un-marriage; we should, for balance, mention un-singleness.

OK, let's look at why people pursue marriage. The reasons are as numerous as the shifting sands- love, romance, sex, family and stability. These reasons, as worthy as they may be, all are slightly esoteric and have feelings as the main element. Let's take a look at the original reason marriage was invented, then maybe some of the emotional motivations will come into better focus. God wanted Adam to have a helpmate or, using a more contemporary term, a teammate.[22]

Synergy

When teams work together, they exhibit synergy – where the sum is greater than its parts. This synergy takes a shared vision of two separate people and multiplies it. "And ye shall chase your enemies, and they shall fall before you by the sword. And five of you shall chase a hundred, and a hundred of you shall chase ten thousand; and your enemies shall fall before you by the sword. And I will have respect unto you, and make you fruitful, and multiply you, and will establish my covenant with you."[23]

Not to get too theological, but this seems to suggest a spiritual principle where with God, five warriors can thwart a hundred warriors. That's a pretty good average – one fighter defeating twenty. But, look what happens when a hundred warriors with shared vision fight. They chase down TEN THOUSAND enemy fighters. Just like Israel's enemies in this story became aware of this spiritual principle, so too are our enemies today. Any tyrannical leader in history knew that if he didn't find a way to control the people he was oppressing, they would find their teammates and rise up in a common goal to defeat him.

God knew that by building synergistic family units through marriage, He would have a team or an army if He chose to use it.

God's enemy, the devil, also realized that God was building human fortification through marriage. So, he began devising schemes of his own to thwart God's plans. A particularly insidious control method the devil uses is a mind-warp, which weakens God's spiritual principle of synergy. It's called illusion.

Illusion or false identity comes from our enemies – Satan, the world system and our own carnal nature. Culture, societal expectations, verbal abuse, self-centeredness, selfishness, iniquity, sin, Satan all can distort how we see ourselves.

Let's say, God purposed Melissa to be an architect. "Before I formed thee in the belly I knew thee, and before thou camest forth out of the womb I sanctified thee; I have appointed thee a prophet unto the nations."[24]

Melissa was young and in her first drafting class. Her ill-tempered instructor made a mockery of her for some of her avant-garde designs in front of the whole class. She never returned to drafting class. Poor Melissa never learned technical drawing. She instead became the world's most fastidious chambermaid.

In Melissa's class was a young man named Edgar. Ed didn't laugh when the teacher mocked Melissa. His dream was to build. Because Melissa was mortified, she never returned to class. She missed meeting Edgar. The two of them together would have developed gym equipment for the mentally and physically disabled – things never before imagined would have been used to benefit millions of developmentally challenged people worldwide.

Melissa believed the illusion perpetrated by her instructor that her ideas were strange and stupid. She was pushed off her perfect destiny path by her enemy – a man's carnal ego, belittling her to make himself feel important.

As an illusion is built within us, the synergy of any team, including marriage, begins to tear down. We have purpose, destiny and identity in God. If we begin to believe less than this, then we begin to weaken the spiritual synergy.

<u>Fear and Discouragement</u>
Even in the best of environments, unmarried people can still fear being or staying single. We just don't want to live life alone.

The feelings related to loneliness like pain, discouragement and fear are all forms of inebriation used by your enemy to further the illusion that you are indeed alone. "If only I could be married to The One, then I could love and be loved."

There are few worse ways to choose a mate than out of loneliness. And, marriage certainly is not a cure for it. Marriage may cure alone-ness, but many married folks are just as lonely, some even more so, than some of us singles. Listen to any good country ballad if you need further explanation on the difference between loneliness and being alone.

Singled In can make sure we singles are neither lonely nor alone. You are already loved. Right now. To borrow a line from Christian singer John Cox, "Someone loved you, loved you to death," as he describes Jesus' sacrifice on the cross so that you may be together with your Heavenly Father forever.[25] "...for he hath said, I will never leave thee, nor forsake thee."[26] Your cure for loneliness is in God. Your relationship with Him will reap many rewards, including having Him as a constant companion.

Beware of the illusions of success, including those of marriage, family, career or even church. The world would have you believe that feelings of fulfillment can be had if only you make the right choices. You don't need God for that. The truth is that even though successes in marriage, family, career and church are laudable, they should flow from your personal relationship with God. Allow Him to strip away any illusion associated with them. In other words, become disillusioned. It's a good thing.

A Good Thing

Disillusionment...is not discouragement. In fact, disillusionment is the goal. Our identities are IN Christ. There is no illusion in Christ. We are to strive to see without blinders or scales on our spiritual eyes.

When I was a child, I believed Santa Claus somehow fit down a chimney. Now, I know he uses elves to do the dirty work. I became disillusioned and now, I see clearly.

As a youth, I dreamed of being a baseball player, a rock star and a millionaire. Jethro Bodine (of the TV show *Beverly*

Hillbillies) had a similar fantasy. "Uncle Jed, I don't know whether I wants to be a brain surgeon, a double naught spy or a fry cook." Jethro and I both travailed under our illusions. I'm not sure what star Jethro eventually followed, but for me, I believe I've cracked it this time. I'm sure that being a book-writing whale farmer is what God wants me to be. I see clearly now, without the prejudice of illusions.

All joking aside, I hope you see my point. Everything we allow to enter our world can effect the way we see ourselves. For better or worse, we shape our self-image and our purpose using the input of the world in which we live.

God, however, is constantly trying to get our attention. Our world is so hectic and full of distraction, it is easy to miss His "still small voice."[27] Sometimes, we need to get alone in a quiet zone to "Be still and know..." that He is God.[28] Other times, we need to change our perception from an linear, earthly understanding to more of an encompassing, heavenly one.

Even if we find ourselves in the throes of contemporary electronic living, He can still visit us in our dreams. In her excellent book, *Seeing the Voice of God*, bestselling author, Laura Harris Smith makes the case that God is never silent.[29] He uses the time that our bodies are resting to speak to our spirits.

He says, "Do you not perceive? Do you not understand? This is how I see you. As a lump of clay, the potter sees nothing but potential. When I put My hands to it, all of that potential comes to life with form, breath, power, purpose and destiny. Through the bloody veil of My Son's sacrifice, you look just like Jesus to Me. He had a purpose on earth and so do you."

To become truly dis-illusioned, we must grab hold of how God sees us. Oswald Chambers writes in *My Utmost for His Highest*,

"In the beginning Moses realized that he was the one to deliver the people, but he had to be trained and disciplined by God first. He was right in his individual perspective, but he was not the person for the work until he had learned true fellowship and oneness with God.

We may have the vision of God and a very clear understanding of what God wants, and yet when we start to do it, there comes to us something equivalent to Moses' forty years in the wilderness. It's as if God had ignored the entire thing, and when we are thoroughly discouraged, God comes back and revives His call to us."[30]

As I mentioned earlier, there are myriad reasons why people want to marry. I have some good friends, who have done some pre-marital counseling with couples. They sit down with them and discuss the reasons why the couple wants to marry. And, in good counseling fashion, offer levelheaded advice and pragmatic vision rooted in experience.

Some couples respond well and take into account the sage wisdom of experts in the field. However, there are many couples who, if they do any counseling at all, treat it more like a pre-requisite course to be checked off the list. They tend to rush into marriage, because the thought and thrill help facilitate an illusion of happiness and fulfilled dreams that they have for themselves.

Yes, of course, marriage can foster sustained happiness and even fulfill dreams, but any successfully married couple will tell you how much work is involved to reach those plateaus. That synergy we discussed earlier isn't magically going to happen after "I do." Every enemy of God's Kingdom is put on notice when two people begin to walk together in His name and for His sake. The resistance is persistent. But, for those called into marriage, the pay-off in purpose is pure poetry.

I went for the alliteration over depth of meaning in that last sentence. My point is that if God's perfect will is for you to be married, it is within that journey where you will find your peak pick of spiritual fruit. And, along that path as you submit to His testing, any self-identity illusions will be replaced by the ultimate image found in Jesus.

"That the communication of thy faith may become effectual by the acknowledging of every good thing which is in you in Christ Jesus"[31]

The One

This is far from being a how-to guide to finding a mate. We're here to maximize the fulfillment found in being *Singled In* to your community. However, as a free service to those of you who know for a fact that God's perfect will for you is marriage, here's a helpful tip to help you to know for sure when you have found "The One." Are you ready? Here it is:

After being in a relationship of mutual physical attraction and respect, "The One" is that one person who supports your walk and whose walk you can support without compromising God or yourself.

He/she will be both your best teammate and your best cheerleader. At least, that's how I see it. But, remember, this definition is coming from a guy who has been unmarried for over fifty years. So, grab the saltshaker and be as liberal with it as you please.

14

The Advantages

Paul calls it "a gift"

<u>Accentuate the Positive</u>

A *Singled In* ministry is one of inclusion. Unmarried persons need not be pitied or denigrated. Instead, they are to be honored as any other person. Encourage them where they are as unmarried people, but, in the spirit of *Singled In*, make that encouragement toward God's perfect will for their lives. Remember Paul's advice to, "Let each man abide in that calling wherein he was called."[32] Being single is as much a calling as is being married.

If marriage is part of that calling, a.k.a. perfect will, then a *Singled In* participant will already be on the road to maturity and preparedness for the occasion. In either case, live a life that makes God proud to show you off. A quick read through Ephesians chapter 4 will show what that will take.

I am very aware of certain predilections towards matchmaking out there. It's gratifying to see two people meet and grow together. Some even find fun in it. I don't want to spoil anyone's good time, but let me share a caution with you as a witness to some well-intentioned matchmaking. Take a moment before saying something like, "Hey, I know this great guy" or "I think she likes you" to someone. You may inadvertently side track a single just discovering their identity in Christ. Or, they may be on a solemn healing path for a time. Just be aware that there are purposes to being single and a new co-ed relationship may not fit into that present purpose.

But, by all means, encourage these singles you love to use their gifts to help others and by reminding them of the promises of God. In so doing, confidence and purpose will begin to flow, in them and in you.

Unmarried Bible Characters

We've mentioned the Bible quite a bit. Its principles were used to form and govern our life in the United States. So, it's fair to say that it is quite useful as our moral compass. Many in today's amoral society are searching for deeper meaning, so let's grab a Bible and look at some examples of success stories – unmarried people *Singled In* by God.

For those of you new to Bible study, you may run across a group of people in the Old Testament called the Hittites (pronounced Hit'•tites). They are in no way to be confused with Hotties (pronounced Hot'•ties). Although unconfirmed, the groups are thought to not be mutually exclusive and thus, awareness may aid to avoid confusion - just a head's up.

OK. Now we're ready for an historical perspective. Let's look at those single people in the Bible.

Isaac, son of Abraham, was single until he was 40 years old and represents the gold standard for waiting on God's perfect will. The 67 verses of Genesis chapter 24 detail the amazing and romantic tale.

Miriam was Moses' eldest sister, a Prophetess and dancing worshipper in Ex 15:20; and a respected leader in Num 12:5.

Samson was a Nazarite, chosen by God to do holy work as one of Israel's first Judges (Jud 13-16). But, the word Nazarite also means "an untamed vine." And, he was most assuredly that as well. He followed his fancy and his hormones most of his life. Ole Sammy may have even inspired Paul to write 1 Cor 7:9. Even so, he is used as a archetype of Christ by theologians like Robert Hawker (*Poor Man's Commentary*) and Matthew Henry in *Commentary of the Whole Bible* "...but the truth is Samson was himself a riddle, a paradox of a man, did that which was really great and good, by that which was seemingly weak and evil, because he was designed not to be a pattern to us (who must walk by rule, not by example), but a type of him who, though he knew no sin, was made sin for us, and appeared *in the likeness of sinful flesh,* that He might *condemn* and *destroy sin in the flesh,* Rom 8:3."

Four of Israel's major prophets were unmarried – Elijah, Elisha, Jeremiah and Daniel. Even Daniel's young friends, Shadrach, Meshach, Abednego – the righteous royals, all led quite powerful and adventurous lives.

John the Baptist, the Apostle John, Mary Magdalene and Lazarus were not only single, but singular witnesses to Jesus (who was also single) and His ministry.

The Apostle Paul, Barnabas, Timothy and a wealthy businesswoman named, Lydia (Acts 16:14, 40) used the gift of singleness to promote The Way to the corners of the earth.

Better Than Marriage

Whether single-for-life or between marriages, being unmarried has advantages. Those advantages can be found while serving the Lord free from distraction.[33] When you read this letter of Paul's to the Corinthians, remember that he is writing to a specific group of people with specific challenges. Apparently, the church in Corinth needed some guidance in regards to marriage.

To get a more complete view of how Paul viewed marriage, in Eph 5:32 he embraces it as a lofty notion that symbolizes Christ's love for His church. So, he clearly believes in the institution of marriage. He seems to caution the Corinthians saying in effect, "be sure you're ready for the institution before you become institutionalized." <You didn't realize a single Christian guy could be so snarky, did you? >

Singled In puts its participants into position to discover and use all the advantages found in serving the Lord free from distraction to the benefit of all. If your fellowship or civic group is not practicing *Singled In*, you may be under-serving your unmarried population to your own detriment. Exercise the advantages of your unmarried folks and watch while everyone benefits as your group grows.

Unfortunately, the advantages being underserved within church walls are not lost on the world outside. The world has certainly found ways to focus and capitalize. Singleness is celebrated with ads, products and media promoting promiscuity, debauchery and altered states.

Of course, society has more products to sell when this salacious lifestyle proves its predictable consequences. In less complicated times, the church's answer to temptations like these has been marriage. And, for many years, this approach worked. These days with population growth and nuclear family deterioration, *Singled In* suggests that our singles' growth and contribution in God's big happy family should also be vigorously encouraged.

15

The Sex and the Sin

Premarital sex is fun

<u>But, if we love each other...</u>

Most unmarried people run into a prevailing sentiment. This unspoken sentiment sometimes becomes a very spoken question, "So, why aren't you married yet?" I have heard this from family, friends, barely-acquainted church members and prospective girlfriends.

My answers have run a gamut from, "I'm waiting for God's perfect mate" to "I haven't found one who recognizes God's gifts yet" to "Girls are crazy" to "I've got issues." I am particularly fond of a snarky social media meme that sometimes hits the spot, "Stop asking <u>why</u> I'm single. I don't ask <u>how</u> you're still married."

Unfortunately, I have encountered another reason on more than one occasion, which is worth expounding upon.

Our society has embraced pre-marital sex as a norm. It is sad that this level of moral decline is so prevalent, but if we take a brief browse through end-times scripture, it should come as no shock. What does surprise me is that so many good church-going folks would allow themselves to believe that sex outside of marriage is acceptable. It goes to show that Justification-ism is still quite active and secular society is still a quite potent director of moral decay.

When I met Holy Spirit in the balcony of that church (Chap 7), I was not living the moral life I am living and espousing now. My girlfriend and I were "playing house." (I hope this well-worn euphemism makes its point.) Once I encountered His holiness, I became convicted of my behavior, repented and sought change. After I received the dramatic answer to my prayer, I vowed that I would never allow myself to "play house" again. Beyond choosing God's wisdom by being obedient to His law, choosing God's plan for sex has benefits that outweigh those found in our carnal desire.

"So, what is God's plan for sex? Sex is fun. Just watch movies and TV. Ask anyone. Why is it forbidden? Doesn't God want us to enjoy ourselves?"

Sex is a precious gift, intended for those who would commit to God and to each other to love in a triple braided chord for life.

There were a few things not included in God's rough draft of *Life With Humans*. He did some page crumpling after the Adam/Eve/apple thing. I'm not saying God didn't know that free will wouldn't affect His perfect plan. He knows the end from the beginning.[34] And, let's save the theological predestination debate for another time. For our purposes with *Singled In*, I contend that His perfect plan was rocking along in the Garden until the Adams family forced Plan B into effect.

It can be argued that Adam and Eve were intended to be in Eden with God forever. They would follow God's command to "Be fruitful and multiply…" and sexually produce a family, a nation and, eventually, a world.[35]

No sin. No death. No knowledge of evil. The happy people would live their lives in an earthly paradise experiencing a euphoric state of being and feeling.

It started out that way for Adam and Eve, but…

…then sin occurred and changed everything. God expelled the Adams family from the paradise He created for them. And, with the expulsion came curses. In application, these curses came upon all three parties involved – man, woman and serpent. Each was separated from God in a unique way.

(I didn't include Lucifer in my list of the accursed. He had previously been cursed and expelled from heaven at this point in linear history. But, the poor serpent that Lucifer used to perpetrate his deception upon Eve lost his legs in the debacle.)

For our two humans, there would be no more nakedness without shame. No more prosperity without work. No more life without death. No more reproduction without pain. And, no more bliss without commitment. The new life would be a shadow of the old and that only through blood, sweat and tears. The couple would need to work hard and continually to find glimpses of that original happiness again.

Since the Eden eviction, the purpose of the physical act of sex has not changed. It is still a celebration of two bodies, two souls and two spirits becoming one with each other and God: heralding the beginning of procreation.

But, in a post-sin world, the sexual experience is a mere shadow of the original euphoria. His perfect will was for Adam and Eve to walk together in bliss with Him in His Garden...for as long as He wanted. The relationship between the three was sacred. Sex, being a testimony to this relationship, is still to be set apart (sacred) for use in the holy ordinance of marriage. Only then can it be fully appreciated.

When my friends the marriage counselors spoke with loving couples before the nuptials, they most assuredly told the couple that marriage is more than what is commonly believed. To God and to each spouse, marriage is a covenant, which includes promises and legal binding. The promises include all three parties – husband, wife and God. Physical intimacy between the couple also includes three parts – body, soul and spirit. Sex serves as the covenant's consummation and testifies that a marriage has occurred, where two persons have become one. "Therefore shall a man leave his father and his mother, and shall cleave unto his wife: and they shall be one flesh."[36] The word "consummate" itself exemplifies two becoming one as the new creation consumes each mate.

We use much less intimate forms of this consummation example everyday when we shake hands. The physical flesh-to-flesh act testifies to a meeting between persons. The gesture, through physical touch, captures the personalities, intent and bond between the parties. "You can tell a lot about a person by their handshake."

<u>Cause to Celebrate</u>

The reason a ceremony still exists to celebrate marriage is many-fold. Although the covenant is made between the couple and God, outside witnesses are asked to participate to hear the words being spoken and hold the couple accountable to those things promised to each other and to God. These spoken words serve as a foundation upon, which the marriage is built. It is essential for the relationship to be reminded of these foundations – God, spouses or witnesses.

Sex by a married couple bears witness to the promises they made to each other and to God. As a result, those bonds are strengthened. They include the physical (finding each other attractive), emotional (keeping promises) and spiritual (allowing God to be head of the relationship).

When sex happens outside of the bonds of marriage, the consummation process still occurs, because, in effect, a marriage has still occurred. Sex is the physical act that testifies to a marriage – two becoming one. And, whether implicit or explicit the intent of the act is interpreted by body, soul and spirit as a covenant relationship. If, however, no covenant was intended, the couple engaged in intimacy has metaphorically signed a blank marriage license. The names of the participants are on the page, but the words spelling out the covenant are waiting to be written.

As any good businessperson knows, no one should sign his or her name to a blank piece of paper. There is just no way to control what may get written into the contract above the signature line. This is what happens with sex outside of covenant-marriage. Each person signs his or her name and the blank contract begins filling up. Instead of the agreement being filled with thoughtful and binding words spoken at a ceremony, every physical, emotional and spiritual relationship, past and present, is invited into the couple's new arrangement.

This same couple, had they consummated a covenant-marriage properly, would still have all of the same past and present relationships entering into their new marriage, but they would be covered by the grace, mercy, blood and redemption of Jesus to work all things to the good (Rom 8:28). Without this inclusion and covering of God, a sex relationship without covenant can become chaotic very quickly.

Is it any wonder then that participants in casual sex with multiple partners often have frenzied, foundationless, unfulfilling relationships? These sinful episodes cause whirlwinds of emotion and physiological desires exposing the true wanton need for a firm foundation and ultimately a

Savior. They sure make for some pitiful, yet entertaining afternoon television, though.

Purity

Purity then, is the key element to enjoying the elation that Adam and Eve did simply while walking with God in the Garden. As we've established, until Satan the Sinful Snake entered into convivial conversation with Mrs. Adams, there was no sin in man. Adam and Eve were so pure; they had no knowledge of evil. They were naked and felt no shame. They obeyed God in the simplicity of their innate desire to be in His presence and do what pleased Him. We can suppose then that they had no desire or need to have sex.

Purpose of sex

Do you see the intended purpose of sexual intimacy coming into focus? God wants couples to enjoy intimacy with each other. With body, soul and spirit all involved, the act alone reminds human kind of what must have been overwhelming feelings of love and belonging we once had in the Garden with God.

He still enjoys walks with us in the garden during the cool of the day and longs for closeness with us. He had to design a new way in the post-sin world. A strenuous act replaced a leisurely walk. Brief moments replaced abiding contentment. Yet, His desire is for couples to know these things and recognize that it was He that gave them as part of His abundant life package.

In this way, sex strengthens the bond between God, man and woman – a picture of a Garden walk. It may even be said that the reason God romanticizes these walks in Eden so much is that they are the reason He took time to build this planet and make people-shaped mud pies in the first place.

As we discussed earlier, another of the purposes of sexual intimacy is to re-create man in God's own image. Each new baby's face shows another shining facet of God's.

I Can't Wait

The intended environment of sexual intimacy is one of purity of body, soul and spirit, complete trust with one's spouse and an innate desire to be one with them.

I hear you thinking. "Well, saving sex until marriage may be God's perfect will, but I don't want to wait. On this issue, I'll just settle for His acceptable will and a double helping of grace."

Unfortunately for purity's sake, this is an extremely prevalent attitude, which begins in what Paul calls one's "carnal man" and is fueled by popular culture and the absence of over-sight and/or accountability.

It is also unfortunate that, if someone thinks about pre-marital sex at all, it is quite doubtful that God's will – perfect or otherwise, factors into the process. The fact is that pre-marital sex is sin. Sin is not acceptable to God.

Adultery – Plain and Simple

Sex, as outlined above, was made for heterosexual couples in a binding, committed marriage.

Exhibit "1" from the Ten Commandments: "Thou shalt not commit adultery."[37] The Hebrew word for adultery means "a woman who breaks wedlock."

Exhibit "2" from moral law: "And the man that committeth adultery with *another* man's wife, *even he* that committeth adultery with his neighbour's wife, the adulterer and the adulteress shall surely be put to death."[38]

Exhibit "3" from Jesus: "But I say unto you, That whosoever looketh on a woman to lust after her hath committed adultery with her already in his heart."[39]

Exhibit "4" from Paul: "Now the works of the flesh are manifest, which are *these;* Adultery, fornication, uncleanness, lasciviousness, idolatry, witchcraft, hatred, variance, emulations, wrath, strife, seditions, heresies, envyings, murders, drunkenness, revellings, and such like: of the which I tell you before, as I have also told *you* in time past, that they which do such things shall not inherit the kingdom of God."[40]

Now, I hear you thinking "but we love each other. I KNOW that we will be married one day. We just want to show our love for each other and sex is the best way to do it."

Well, until you ARE married, legally, spiritually and morally, your sex partner is actually someone's husband-to-be or wife-to-be. Adultery - plain and simple.

Remember, you're thinking out loud to a man who is a reformed Justification-ist. I'd say with your thoughts of "sex before marriage is OK if you love each other," we shared the same pew at our Church of Justification. "This thought process shows no courage, discipline, forethought or concern for anyone other than your self and your own self-gratification," said the pot to the kettle.

"But, what about the Old Testament guys, who had multiple wives and concubines. That seemed to work out OK."

Just because someone made the cut into the canonized Bible, does not make him or her sinless. (See King David or Samson). Abraham was the first Bible character to have a mistress or concubine. In Hebrew grammar, the word "concubine" doesn't even have a root. The word and practice were borrowed from other cultures, like the Egyptians, Assyrians and Babylonians. Although inconclusive, this fact points toward God's original one-woman-for-one-man template.

Abram and wife Sarai were both "well-stricken in age" and childless when they, without God's direction, decided to create for themselves a legacy. With his wife's blessing, Abram impregnated an Egyptian servant girl. The conspiracy, although producing a male heir, was sinful. The marriage bond had been broken.

And, like a soap opera drama, as soon as Hagar the Egyptian servant girl began to show, Sarai began to jealously hate her. There were also many longer-term consequences to this extramarital tryst.

God had a plan for Abram and Sarai. He wanted to surprise them with it, but their impatience sullied the gift. When Ishmael, Abram's son by Hagar, was thirteen, God appeared to Abram with His surprise – a covenant. The Almighty would build a people and plant them in the land of Canaan forever using the Abram family as forbearers. In return for the land grant and a lineage that would include kings and many nations, these people would venerate God as their own, forever. To consummate the covenant, God instituted the act of circumcision, which would be a recurring sign throughout the generations. As a bonus, living prophetic signs were established when God changed Abram's name to Abraham and Sarai's name to Sarah to reflect the new "parents of many nations" status.

To recap using mathematics:

Abraham + Sarah + son^y X land^z = God's plan (His perfect will)

(where ^{y} = Jewish nation and ^{z} = Canaan)

Because The Abram's grew impatient thirteen years earlier with the couple's own vision of legacy, Ishmael became a factor in a new equation (son^x). Abram loved his son and beseeched God to bless him, which He did. God blessed Ishmael with his own lineage of princes and made him a great (elder brother) nation – clearly not as an abundant a blessing as Abraham's younger son, Isaac was to enjoy.

Like the sin in Eden's Garden, the sin in Hagar's tent bred consequences that last to this day. Ishmael did indeed become an elder nation – that of modern day Arabs – a largely Muslim population. Since Ishmael was not given a land grant, he, through his progeny, still fights to have a home. With the rage of an older brother scorned of his birthright, Ishmael is jealous for Father Abraham's blessing, like Isaac and Israel (Jacob) received.

Thousands of years of unrest in the Middle East could have been prevented had one couple stayed true to their marriage vows; asked for God's guidance and encouragement; then waited for His perfect will.

Sex, like natural beauty, wisdom or peace is a gift from God, because He loves you. If nurtured, protected and enjoyed within the bounds established by their Creator, His gifts can add ever-growing elements of enjoyment and fulfillment to your life. Like any Christmas gift, it is up to you to what degree. It can be cherished and used appropriately or abused and thrown into a corner.

Sin Misses the Mark

Picture an archery target. The bull's eye is God's perfect will. The next larger ring is His good will. And, the next larger ring is His acceptable will. If you're like me, I'm such a bad shot; my arrows tend to stick not in the target at all, but into the wall on which the target is hanging. After years and years of shooting those "sin" arrows into the wall, the wall itself begins to deteriorate and break apart. The sheet rock crumbles until a wall barely exists. God's will target soon falls through the wall to where it can't even be seen any longer.

God loves the world He created and all of the people He placed within it. He wants everyone to spend eternity with Him. He also knows that Adam and Eve, before they sinned, are the only two human beings who looked Him in the eye and survived to tell the tale. After sin, no one could gaze upon His face without being destroyed. God is the essence of purity and righteousness. If anything less presents itself to Him, it cannot survive.

He remedied that situation when He sent His son, Jesus, to interact with us. Jesus told us all about our Father God and showed us what our Father did out of love for us. Through His Son's sacrifice, Father God removed our sin and made the way for us to live again with Him in His heavenly Eden.

If you allow Him to do so, Jesus, will slowly tear out the old, ragged mess of a wall and replace it with all new sheet rock. He will pull out old arrows, patch the holes with mud and sand them until they're smooth again.

He longs to do this same thing for all of us, no matter how badly we have missed that target or for how long. An important distinction is that God loves us – the beings that He created. He doesn't love what we do – good or bad. God loves a person, knowing that the person has sinned and will do so again. In effect, our actions, just like we discussed in the marriage scenario above, testify to our relationship with God. If we sin, we are given a choice by our Maker to either repent (turn away) of that action and shoot another arrow at the target, or just keep shooting at the wall. If we continue with our sin behavior, we are testifying that we are choosing our selves and our actions over our relationship with God.

We are all sinners in need of a savior to keep us from going to hell. "...for all have sinned, and fall short of the glory of God."[41]

Every single person's purpose is to glorify God. Nothing accomplishes this more readily than rejecting our own sinful desires and following His directives. "For this, Thou shalt not commit adultery, Thou shalt not kill, Thou shalt not steal, Thou shalt not covet, and if there be any other commandment, it is summed up in this word, namely, Thou shalt love thy neighbor as thyself. Love worketh no ill to his neighbor: love therefore is the fulfillment of the law."[42]

16

The Conclusion

Being single is a gift – not a curse

The inclusion of unmarried people into the fabric of community serves both the individual and the community.

A single person has an ability to serve God with an undivided heart and therefore should be supported and encouraged to do so. Through the journey as a single, many potential mates will arise. If it is God's purpose for one of those potentials to become the mate, it will happen as both move forward in God's plan for each. To force the issue will only cause both to fall short of potential. Of course, God is The Redeemer and can intervene in any relationship to His glory. But one should strive for His perfect will, not just His acceptable or good will.

Singled In is a mindset

Being single is not a curse. It is a state of being that may be uncomfortable, at times, but not one to be a continuing source of discouragement, pain, fear or loneliness. It is popular social science to prescribe "community" to those who feel ostracized. *Singled In* is an approach to involving unmarried (never-married and single-again) people of all ages into the fabric of "community." Although, the approach can be adapted into secular society via government, civic and faith-based programs, it's strongest and best use is in the church dynamic.

Just for kicks, let's see if our friends Joan and Nadine from The First Bapticostal, etc. Church have been reading along with you and paying attention to our *Singled In* idea...

Our Lady of the Hard Head

Wednesday night arrives. Nadine has been anxiously waiting for Joan to appear in the church doorway. A wet, chilly draft ushers Joan into the foyer.

"Joanie!"

"Well, hello Nadine. You're here early tonight. Did you have another pastor-adjustment meeting with Brother Bill or did you just get locked in on Sunday?" Nadine was feeling her oats.

"Very funny, Joan. I'll have you know that pastor needs a little adjustin' up in here some times. Now listen, I wanted to fill you in on the dinner party."

"Help me, Lord." Joan knew that when Nadine got a hold of something, she was like a Rottweiler with a rawhide.

"I called Darlene and invited her on Saturday night. I got some sparkle juice, and Sinatra pipin' in through the air vents. I need your help. What do you suppose lovebirds like to eat?" Nadine was in the zone.

"I got a better idea. I told the *Singled In* group leader that you were an old woman and needed lots of help around your place..."

"Ahhhh..." Nadine's overly dramatic shock was expected. "You didn't!"

"I did," Joan continued. "And, you know what? Those two, along with some other good single folk from the church will be showing up at your house Saturday morning. They'll be cuttin' your grass, cleanin' your gutters and takin' that old TV to the recyclers for you."

Nadine was blindsided. "How is that a better idea? Jeffrey and Darlene might not even see each other in all that ruckus."

Joan and Nadine would certainly benefit from being *Singled In* themselves. It might, at least, open up possibilities for new hobbies.

"Nadine, sometimes you can be so thick. They'll be all day over at your house working with each other and everyone else. They'll be able to let their guards down and just be themselves. If they start sparkin' nothin' says you can't fan the flames a little."

"Joanie, I swear if I didn't love you so much I'd punch you in the neck. That ain't how it's done. Now you call the whole thing off and get Jeffrey on over here for dinner Saturday night."

"I won't." Joan packed her powder and stood ramrod straight as she loaded for another shot.

Nadine, just as defiantly turned and walked toward her classroom hurling her words off of the brico blocks and linoleum, "And another thing, what gives a person the right to tell anybody I'm an old lady who can't take care of herself? And I'm gonna sell that TV. Somebody'll take it. And, my grass-cuttin' guy hurt his foot and can't mow this week..." Her words trailed off as she turned the corner.

Joan, left standing in a cold puddle, still in the foyer yelled after the mule-headed heretic, "I never told them you were an old <u>lady</u>..." then only loud enough for herself to hear, "...I said old <u>woman</u>. There's a difference you daft..."

Clearly, Joan got the *Singled In* memo after Sunday's service and is trying to put it into practice. As you can see, her efforts are meeting with some resistance, as traditions are sometimes hard to overcome. But, with patience and persistence, any good idea will eventually take root, even in the driest and hardest of soils.

Using a *Singled In* mindset will help any truth seeker find self-fulfillment and purpose as he/she serves others. So, include singles of all ages in community events. We are brothers and sisters and should be treated as such. If marriage is part of the plan, being *Singled In* is a healthy way to explore and discover.

So, whether it's a friend, a romantic interest or Jesus Himself, with whom you spend your time, your mate awaits! But, whoever it is, keep Him, him or her waiting no longer. Get *Singled In*!

NOTES

1. Page 29 - Josh Harris, *I Kissed Dating Goodbye* (Multnomah Books, 1997)
2. Page 30 - Luke 1:37 KJV
3. Page 36 - 2 Cor 4:7 ASV
4. Page 39 - Rom 12:2 ASV
5. Page 40 – John 10:10 KJV
6. Page 40 – Rom 8:29 ASV amplified
7. Page 41 – Matt 6:33 KJV paraphrased
8. Page 42 – Rom 12:2 ASV
9. Page 62 - **JENGA®** is a registered trademark owned by Pokonobe Associates. © 2014 Pokonobe Associates. All rights reserved.
10. Page 72 – Super Bowl® is a registered trademark of the NFL and is used as nominative fair use with no association between author or publisher expressed or implied
11. Page 75 – Ecc 8:1 ASV
12. Page 77 – Ps 16:5 ASV paraphrased
13. Page 77 – John 15:5 ASV
14. Page 82 – Gen 2:18 ASV
15. Page 83 – Matt 6:33 KJV
16. Page 91 – I Cor 7:32-35 ASV
17. Page 101 – Ep 3:19 ASV
18. Page 104 – Star Trek® is a registered trademark of Paramount Pictures Corporation
19. Page 106 – John 21:17 KJV
20. Page 114 – Jer 29:11 ASV paraphrased
21. Page 121 – Zech 4:10 ASV paraphrased
22. Page 129 - Gen 2:20 ASV paraphrased
23. Page 129 – Lev 26:7-9 ASV
24. Page 131 – Jer 1:5 ASV
25. Page 134 – John Cox, " Child Again" from *80 Years* (Up A Tree, 2000)
26. Page 134 – Heb 13:5 KJV
27. Page 136 – 1 Kings 19:12 KJV
28. Page 136 – Ps 46:10 KJV paraphrased
29. Page 136 – Laura Harris Smith, *Seeing the Voice of God* (Chosen Books, 2014)
30. Page 137-138 – Oswald Chambers, *My Utmost for His Highest* (Public Domain, 1924)
31. Page 139 - Philemon 1:6 KJV
32. Page 142 – 1 Cor 7:20 ASV
33. Page 147 – 1 Cor 7:32 ASV paraphrased
34. Page 152 – Rev 22:13 ASV
35. Page 152 – Gen 1:28 KJV
36. Page 155 – Gen 2:24 KJV
37. Page 162 – Ex 20:14 KJV
38. Page 162 – Lev 20:10 KJV
39. Page 162 – Matt 5:28 KJV
40. Page 162-163 – Gal 5:19-21 KJV
41. Page 170 – Rom 3:23 ASV
42. Page 170 – Rom 13:9-10 ASV

43. Page 180 - Jeffrey Lee Brothers has been a compensated endorser of Warrior Musical Instruments, Rossville, GA since 1999

ABOUT THE AUTHOR

It was a wet and windy Tuesday night in March when David Janssen was nearly apprehended again during a gripping episode of *The Fugitive*. VCR was more than a decade away from being invented, so it was hang onto your water or wait for the re-run. A few hours later, baby Jeffrey bounced into the world. Mama had to wait until late summer to see if Dr. Kimble had eluded capture and gathered more evidence on the one-armed man.

The stories embedded in *Singled In* snapshot Jeffrey's life through the mid 2000's. Since then, he helped build a record label, a few music publishing companies and a couple of books on the history of Contemporary Christian Music entitled *Hot Hits*.

In addition, he has done a bit of background acting in two feature length films, a few music videos, some promotional reels, dinner theater, Church dramas and a network TV show.

But, his greatest loves are spending time with family and friends; especially nephews and godchildren. And, worshipping Jesus with his Warrior custom bass.[43]

Photo credit: Kathy Howe Travis

To know more, check out Jeffrey's Facebook author page facebook.com/jbauthorpage, on Twitter @SingledinJLB or http://www.singled-in.net. For personal appearances, email info@singled-in.net

*Braden Scores! (**Singled in** from third) Photo credit: Jeffrey Lee Brothers*

Made in the USA
San Bernardino, CA
01 February 2016